WHAT JESUS DID AND DIDN'T TEACH

by
Conway Dunn

Grosvenor House
Publishing Limited

This book is published by
Grosvenor House Publishing Ltd
Link House
140 The Broadway, Tolworth, Surrey, KT6 7HT.
www.grosvenorhousepublishing.co.uk

A CIP record for this book
is available from the British Library

ISBN 978-1-78623-321-9

Dedication

Once again, my gratitude to Agatha.

About the Author

Conway Dunn is the author of "One Man's Thoughts", a collection of essays mostly philosophical and theological, "The Bible in Worksheets", a participatory, chronological guide, and "We Three Kings", an examination of the reigns of Kings Saul, David and Solomon.

Contents

Introduction

The Purpose   2
The Perimeters   2
The Pitfalls   3

Theology

God   23
Jesus   23
The Holy Spirit   28
The Kingdom of God   30
Salvation   32
Resurrection   36
The Day of Judgement   42
Reward   44
Punishment   45
Theology: a summary   47

Worship

Faith   50
Prayer   51
Fasting   52
Sacrifices   53
The Sabbath   53
Worship: a summary   55

Morality

The Fundamental Commandments   58
The Law   59
Good thoughts and deeds   62
Bad thoughts and deeds   65
Forgiving   66
Enemies   68
Non-resistance   69
Giving   70
Wealth   71
Judging   75
Humility   76
Commitment   78
Divorce   81
Adultery   82
Morality: a summary   82

Particular Groups

The Jewish Leaders   85
Gentiles   86
The Elect   90
Particular Groups: a summary   93

What Jesus Didn't Teach About

The existence of God   95
Politics   95
Human punishments   96
Suicide   98
Abortion   99
Servitude   99
Homosexuality   100
Women   101

Soldiers   103
Animals   104
Topics not taught: a summary   106

A personal perspective   106

Jesus' teaching and Old Testament teaching   115

Introduction

The Purpose

My aim is to find Jesus' fundamental teaching. In the course of this I have detected some ambiguities and variations. I have suggested problems which might arise from certain statements.

There are believers who think that to attribute any difficulties to the Bible and not to ourselves amounts to blasphemy, sceptics who are keen to pinpoint as many difficulties as possible, scoffers who dismiss the whole subject, and a host who are somewhere in between.

I myself write neither in the spirit of adoration nor animosity, but of sincere, open-minded interest. I have strived to identify the relevant details, examine them and offer balanced summaries.

The Perimeters

My boundary is what Jesus himself is purported to have said in the four gospels, Matthew, Mark, Luke and John. I am aware that there are other gospels and apparent words of his in other writings. Within The New Testament are The Acts of the Apostles, the letters and The Revelation to John. These may have drawn upon Jesus' actual teaching (see Acts 20, 35). But I restrict myself to his words as recorded by the four chroniclers approved by the Christian Church.

Even so, I notice differences in the texts cited at the foot of about three-quarters the pages before me. Again, I confine myself to the main text.

I personally do not speak Hebrew, Aramaic or Greek but I have been advised by scholars who do that the most accurate translation of the Bible in English is The

Revised Standard Version so that is the one I use for the readings.

The Pitfalls

The Gospels are biographies of the life of Jesus. In essence they tell the same story - his ministry: teachings, miracles and various events; finally, his trials, execution and resurrection.

There are differences in phrasing, inevitable unless the four authors all used the same source and wrote down word for word exactly what was narrated; and differences in details, most naturally explained by drawing on different sources. Indeed, each gospel has at least one - usually more - complete tale not found in any other; for example, in Matthew, the teaching of the sheep and the goats (25, 31-46), in Mark, a two - fold healing of a blind man (8, 22-26), in Luke, the parable of "the good Samaritan" (10, 30-37) and in John, turning water into wine (2, 1-10). Extra facts provide more knowledge albeit occasionally unremarkable, such as Mark stating that the grass was "green" (6, 39). Sometimes, though, the details disagree with each other. For the substance of the story this may be unimportant. Does it really matter whether Jesus was anointed in the house of Simon the leper (Matt. 26, 6; Mk 14, 3), Simon the Pharisee (Lk 7, 36, 40) or Martha and Mary (Jn 12, 2, 3) or whether Jairus, an official in a Synagogue, came to Jesus when he was "at table" (Matt. 9, 10, 18) or "beside the sea" (Mk 5, 21, 22), or if the "cleansing" of the temple occurred near the beginning (Jn 2,13-16) or near the end (Matt. 21, 12, 13; Mk 11, 15-17; Lk 19, 45, 46) of his ministry? But for the historicity of the gospels the disagreements do matter.

How did they ever arise? Given that not every one of the settings can be correct, either some of the informants were inaccurate, or some of the gospel writers. It may be that the Evangelists received these accounts without a setting and placed them where they thought fit. It all raises the question of the sources' and the authors' personal involvement in the composition and formation of the Gospels.

Assuming nobody wrote down Jesus' words as he spoke them, then the accounts are based on memory. Memory, of course, is limited and fallible. It can forget facts and it can imagine "facts".

No single person or a few people could remember the three chapters (Matt. 5; 6; 7), one hundred and nine verses, of morality delivered at "the sermon on the mount" or the four chapters (Jn 14; 15; 16; 17), one hundred and seventeen verses, of spirituality confided at "the last supper." Regarding "the sermon on the mount" it may be as Luke has it, that the sermon itself was shorter (Lk 6, 20-49), but that Matthew added teachings of Jesus which were actually spoken elsewhere, as Luke has them (e.g. Lk 12, 22-31), but which seemed to slot into the nature of the sermon. Other teachings which might have been grouped together by the authors are some on the subjects of forgiveness (Matt. 18, 15-17, 21-35) and repentance (Lk 15), and the parables of the seeds (Mk 4, 3-9, 14-20, 26-32).

Nonetheless, if it is Luke who is correct about the length of the sermon that still leaves twenty-nine verses (6, 20-49) to be recalled. Would not only all the stipulations, but also all the elaborations be remembered, the six expansions of "giving" described in the first sentence of Luke chapter 6 verse 38, for example?

And memories would probably overlap, both in what they recalled, and in what they forgot, and they would be bitty. So a compiler would need to edit the versions and present his own in complete sentences, and where Jesus' speech is being set out the editing would necessarily involve some reconstruction of his speech. Did Jesus say, "Give to him who begs from you, and do not refuse him who would borrow from you" (Matt. 5, 42) or "Give to everyone who begs from you; and of him who takes away your goods do not ask them again" (Lk 6, 30)?

These problems of memory and the recording of it are likely to occur more the longer the account, so I expect there are many instances within John's four chapters, 14, 15, 16 and 17. It is just too much to accept that over this huge discourse every sentence ostensibly spoken by Jesus was actually spoken by him, especially noting that this subject matter is not specific instructions but interwoven relationships, harder to remember. Further, if Jesus really did say all this, why is more of it not found in the synoptic gospels? Matthew, Mark and Luke have accounts of "the last supper" (Matt. 26, 20-30; Mk 14,17-26; Lk 22, 14-28), but I detect only two episodes mentioned both by them and by John chapters 14-17 - the loss of Judas (e.g. Mk 14, 21. Jn 17,12) and the disciples being with Jesus in his kingdom (e.g. Lk 22, 29, 30. Jn 17, 24). It is quite remarkable that whichever disciple furnished the information about the final evening, which was used by Matthew, Mark and Luke, he said so little about all that John apparently knew. Is a large amount of John chapters 14 - 17 the expoundings of John himself? He was quite prepared to state his own theology (1, 1-18; 3,

16-21, 31-36). He interpreted and developed the words
of Jesus (7, 39) and of the high priest (11, 51, 52),
explained why Isaiah said what he did (12, 41), and
identified points in Jesus' own personality, knowledge
and motives (2, 24, 25; 6, 64; 13, 1,3; 6, 15; 7, 1). Did
he also add his beliefs to Jesus' own words?

One indication that the synoptic writers were prepared to take liberties with the teachings is their use of
so-called "floating verses", that is, sayings which come
in different places in different gospels - for example,
"many that are first will be last, and the last first"
(Matt. 19, 30; Lk 13, 30), "to everyone who has will
more be given" (Matt. 25, 29; Mk 4, 25) and "He
who has ears to hear, let him hear" (Matt. 11, 15; Mk 4,
23). Unless Jesus had a penchant for these remarks and
spoke them on each occasion given, noted by some and
not by others, then the writers or their sources personally inserted a number of them, presumably because
they seemed to reinforce what was being taught.

It might be suggested that extra insertions of Jesus'
statements and, indeed, the adding of new ones are
for the better providing they are consistent with his
teachings in general. But since I am striving to grasp
that teaching, I don't want it to include the musings of
others; no matter how supportive they may seem to be,
they are not his. Some of his apparent statements, when
compared, do not elucidate, but obfuscate. According
to Matthew, Jesus says, "Blessed are the poor in spirit..."
(5, 3) whilst in Luke he says, "Blessed are you poor ..."
(6, 20); again, in Matthew, "Blessed are those who
hunger and thirst for righteousness ..." (5, 6), in Luke,
"Blessed are you that hunger now ..." (6, 21). Matthew
has nine beatitudes (5, 3-12); Luke, four (6, 20-23).

In Matthew's gospel the teaching about what is clean and unclean ends with Jesus listing seven evils (15, 19); in Mark he lists almost twice as many (7, 21, 22). These variations, in meaning or quantity, are considerable and more than I would expect anyone to forget or mistake. It is possible, of course, that the sentences were spoken on separate occasions, but the settings and unfoldings of "the sermon on the mount" accounts in Matthew and Luke are very similar, as are the clean and unclean narratives in Matthew and Mark. Much of the language is also very close. There is no mention of an "again", no hint of a second event. They certainly appear to be descriptions of the same occasion and, if so, the differences outlined are so pronounced I can only conclude someone has purposefully shortened or lengthened Jesus' actual declarations, leaving me not knowing what he really blessed or condemned.

Matthew speaks of spiritually poor (5, 3); Luke of physically poor (6, 20). Again, in Matthew's parable of the marriage feast (22, 2-14) it is the "bad and good" (22, 10) who are gathered; in Luke's parable of the banquet (14, 16-24) it is the "poor and maimed and blind and lame" (14, 21). Luke especially mentions comforting the afflicted and condemning the affluent (see, also, 3, 11; 4, 18; 6, 24, 25; 12, 16-21;14, 13; 16,19-31; 19, 8). These themes seem to be of particular interest to him. In emphasising them did he express his own thoughts amongst those of Jesus? Unique to Luke are the "Woe" verses (6, 24-26) that follow his "Blesseds": woe to the rich and replete, to those who laugh now and who are well-spoken-of. So, wealth is fatal, a grave disposition is necessary and not only conceit but even commendation is bad. Jesus himself seems to have been generally well-spoken-of (e.g. Matt 7, 28, 29; Mk 7, 37; Lk 19, 47, 48; Jn 11, 47,48). It may be that the "woes" are Luke's own opposites of the "Blesseds" and that he overstates the real teachings.

Another theme runs through John's gospel - the need to believe in Jesus, usually that is the phrasing (e.g. 1, 12; 6, 29; 7, 39; 8, 24, 31a; 9, 35; 12, 36; 14, 1; 17, 20; 20, 31), though there are some specific designations, accept him as "the Son of man" (9, 35),"the resurrection and the life" (11, 25), "the light" (12, 36) and "the Christ, the Son of God" (20, 31). "He who believes in the Son has eternal life" (3, 36.Com. 3, 15, 16; 6, 40, 47). "He who does not believe is condemned" (3, 18. Com. 8, 24). Belief, then, is vital. The two quotations just cited and five of the other references given are the words of John. Did he extend his own emphasis on belief into Jesus' speech, especially in the chapters discussed, 14, 15, 16 and 17 (see 14, 1, 12; 16, 9, 27; 17, 8, 20, 21)? The question arises again regarding Jesus living before his earthly life, his pre-existence is another of John's themes (3, 13; 6, 38, 51, 61, 62; 7, 29; 8, 58; 16, 28; 17, 5, 24). Are some of apparently Jesus' sentences really those of John?

A particular case which raises the issue of secondary additions is whether the gospel was intended for Gentiles as well as Jews. Overall, I think it was so meant (see "Gentiles"), but if Jesus made such clear statements as "the gospel must first be preached to all nations" (Mk 13, 10),"repentance and forgiveness of sins should be preached in his name to all nations" (Lk 24, 47) and "go therefore and make disciples of all nations" (Matt. 28, 19), why were "the believers ... amazed" (Acts 10, 45) that Gentiles could become

Christians? Paul and Barnabas turned to non-Jews when the Jews rejected their message (Acts 13, 46) and they supported the expansion by quoting from Isaiah (Acts 13, 47. Isaiah 49, 6). Later, James argued for the inclusion of Gentiles by quoting from "the prophets" (Acts 15, 13-18). Why not draw on one or two of the dozen or so affirmations stated by Jesus himself? Surely there are too many for them all to have been added, or forgotten; some are not bald statements but presented through lengthy stories, such as the parable of the wicked tenants (Mk 12, 1-11). For someone to invent the entire tale, give it a meaning and pretend it was all the work of Jesus would be very audacious. Yet the early church branched out to Gentiles in astonishment and frustration and found succour in the Old Testament instead of in Jesus' own teachings. A real mystery! I wonder, at the least, if some of the seeming declarations of Jesus are really those of the Evangelists or their sources recognising that the church did, in fact, encompass Gentiles and wishing to show that this was at the behest of the Lord.

Accepting differences and acknowledging some secondary overlay, still, it may be claimed, the variant strands can all be brought within the one teaching. Jesus would have blessed the poor in spirit and the poor in body. Supposing Matthew was correct in his list of evils (15, 19), Mark's additional ones (7, 21, 22) would have been sanctioned too. Clearly Jesus was concerned about poverty and illness, and he warned of the perils of riches. Belief is indeed vital. But not all of Mark's extra evils might have been approved - pride can be good as well as bad, and it is strange to call foolishness an evil. In Luke's gospel Jesus implies that the poor will inhabit the kingdom of God (e.g. 6, 20) and the rich will inevitably be rejected (e.g. 6, 24). The first dictum makes no mention of conduct or faith and the second may be too categorical. Considering his teaching on the matter overall, Jesus may have held that wealth was dangerous but not of itself decisive; if so, Luke's pronouncements lead to erroneous conclusions. Belief, but what particular beliefs are essential? Matthew and Luke speak of acknowledging and denying Jesus (Matt. 10, 32, 33; Lk 12, 8, 9), Mark of being ashamed of him (8, 38); however, they don't specify what counts as acceptance or rejection. According to Matthew Jesus instructed that disciples should be baptised "in the name of the Father and of the Son and of the Holy Spirit" (28, 19); according to Luke, Jesus' last words do not include these ones but speak of "repentance and forgiveness" (24, 47), whilst the authenticity of both statements is questionable, as I have just suggested. Apart from Matthew's verse (28, 19), the synoptic writers do not say that Jesus must be given any title. They make only one suggestion of his pre-existence (e.g. Mk 12, 35-37). So they differ from the fourth gospel.

John's repeated declaration that a person needs to believe in Jesus is vague, but where there is detail it seems to include believing that he is the Son of God (e.g. 20, 31). The two apostles on the road to Emmaus spoke of him as "a prophet" (Lk 24, 19). This may be too little. Yet John's insistence on professing him as "the Son", and this a condition for salvation (3, 18), may be too much. John emphasises Jesus' status; the synoptic authors dwell on Jesus' stipulations.

If one also took into account the variations in the text cited at the bottom of the pages, then, of course, there would be more differences, and they are in style and substance. Regarding style, the main narrative of Mark chapter 9 omits verses 44 and 46, presumably to avoid repetition; the same explanation appears to apply to Matthew chapter 12 verse 47. Some writers seemed to consider parts of Matthew chapter 11 verse 15, Mark chapter 2 verse 22 and Luke chapter 12 verse 39 super-fluous, and some that Matthew chapter 6 verse 27, Luke chapter 22 verses 15 and 16 and John chapter 13 verse 10 needed rationalising. Concerning substance, there was an apparent wish to protect Jesus' persona against ignorance (Matt. 24, 36), weakness (Lk 22, 43, 44) and untruthfulness (Jn 7, 8-10). The variation in Matthew chapter 11 verse 12 changes the kingdom of heaven suffering violence to causing it; the one in Luke chapter 17 verse 21 changes the kingdom of God being around you to inside you. If writers were prepared to alter what they found, how many alterations did the Gospel writers themselves make? By adding "without cause" in Matthew chapter 5 verse 22, a requirement virtually impossible to fulfil - never be angry with your "brother" - becomes quite attainable and, indeed, expected - never be angry with your "brother" unless you have a reason. One could amend all of the lofty ideals - never lust, never judge, always turn the other cheek, always give, always forgive, love your enemies - in a similar manner, and bring them down to earth. Is that what Jesus really meant?

Perhaps in "the sermon on the mount", where virtu-ally all of these ideals are to be found, Jesus became too enthused in proclaiming love and his message outstripped his meaning; or his precepts might have been deliberate "sound bites" to make an impact and stimulate thought, containing rather than comprising truth. He did not always speak literally. There are dramatic statements such as, "If your right eye causes you to sin, pluck it out and throw it away" (Matt. 5, 29) and "I have not come to bring peace, but a sword" (Matt. 10, 34); black and white pronouncements such as "all who take the sword will perish by the sword" (Matt. 26, 52) and "he that is not against you is for you" (Lk 9, 50), and unrealistic responses such as, "Leave the dead to bury their own dead" (Lk 9, 60) and "Destroy this temple, and in three days I will raise it up" (Jn 2, 19). Each of these sayings encapsulates a literal concept, but none, I think, is to be taken word for word. Consider, also, "...among those born of women none is greater than John; yet he who is least in the kingdom of God is greater than he" (Lk 7, 28) and "Heaven and earth will pass away, but my words will not pass away" (Lk 21, 33). Truth covered in hyperbole! The ideals could be regarded similarly. They seem to amount to perfection - "You, therefore, must be perfect, as your heavenly Father is perfect" (Matt. 5, 48). But the gospels as a whole do not teach that people should be as perfect as God - far from it - and God and Jesus themselves do not forgive no matter what. At the end of the day there is divine judgement, and this very oration appears to condone human judgement (Matt. 5, 25, 26).

Early in "the sermon" Jesus declares, with the utmost resolution, that nothing in the law will change (Matt. 5, 18); almost immediately he creates a new law (Matt. 5, 22) and changes five (Matt. 5, 27, 28, 31, 32, 33, 34, 38, 39, 43, 44), resulting in two which then demand incredibly unnatural suppression (Matt. 5, 22, 28) and two which then demand an incredibly unnatural reaction (Matt. 5, 39, 44). Clearly, something needs to be changed.

Another occasion when Jesus may have over-stretched his teaching was during "the last supper" when he spoke of the bread as his body and the wine as his blood, according to Matthew (26, 26-28) and Mark (14, 22-24). Luke (22, 17-19) has only the bread reference, whilst John doesn't mention the happening at all. In Matthew and Mark, Jesus says, "This is my blood of the covenant, which is poured out for many" (Matt. 26, 28; Mk 14, 24) and Matthew adds, "for the forgiveness of sins", raising the idea of a sacrifice, suggesting that Jesus by his death takes away the sins of others. The setting was conducive for such a train of thought: Jesus was about to be killed and it was the time of the Passover, when a lamb was sacrificed, so he could be seen as the lamb. But the proposal that he himself removes sin without the sinner acting conflicts with his opening and repeated prescript that people's sins are removed if they repent and change. Perhaps this transformation can be likened to a sacrifice, an act of contrition; the lamb not Jesus' life, but the offerer's old one. He devotes his new one to fulfilling Jesus' teaching. One particular point: in calling the wine his blood and telling his disciples to drink it, he showed scant regard for the commandment not to ingest blood (Leviticus 17, 10-14. Genesis 9, 4). It may be, of course, that he never said these words (Lk 22, 17-19), but assuming that he did since the bread was not his body and the wine was not his blood he was comparing them; perhaps his meaning was that as the disciples absorbed sustenance and it became part of them so they should absorb his teaching, demeanour and purpose until these traits became their very selves. This lesson was particularly important since he was about to leave them. The comparison then underlined that no matter what they were inseparable. They would remain essentially united (com. Jn 14, 20; 15, 4; 17, 21 where they are "in" each other).

Though John's account of "the last supper" does not contain the bread and wine analogy, Jesus - or John - presents it very graphically and publicly earlier in his ministry. Following the feeding of the five thousand (Jn 6, 1-14), Jesus takes up the theme of bread as he had taken up the theme of water with the woman of Samaria (Jn 4, 7-15). Referring to himself as "the bread of life", he speaks of a person coming to him and believing in him (Jn 6, 35) and "he who believes has eternal life" (Jn 6, 47). That is the real teaching (com. Jn 15, 7, 9, 10). But the metaphor of bread is laid and overlaid. He, Jesus, is "the living bread", eat and "live for ever" and the bread is his "flesh" (Jn 6, 51). The Jews take his words literally (Jn 6, 52) and no doubt Jesus adds to their perplexity with "unless you eat the flesh of the Son of man and drink his blood, you have no life in you" (Jn 6, 53).This kind of description fits well with John's emphasis on accepting the person of Jesus; and of God, Jesus and the believers being within one another, but the imagery is so pronounced the hearers may not perceive the meaning. It would have been clearer if the bread had not turned into flesh, and its comparison with the teaching had been expressed as a simile.

To highlight the difficulty in establishing a considerable amount of Jesus' teaching, the following are a list of statements attributed to him which are to some extent at variance with each other:

"Judge not, that you be not judged" (Matt. 7,1) and "judge with right judgement" (Jn 7, 24).

"Whoever divorces his wife and marries another, commits adultery" (Mk 10, 11) and "whoever divorces his wife, except for unchastity, and marries another, commits adultery" (Matt. 19, 9).

"Give to him who begs from you" (Matt. 5, 42) and "you always have the poor with you, and whenever you will, you can do good to them" (Mk 14, 7).

"You know the commandments … 'Honour your father and mother'" (Mk 10, 19) and "If anyone comes to me and does not hate his own father and mother … he cannot be my disciple" (Lk 14, 26).

"...whoever says a word against the Son of man will be forgiven" (Matt. 12, 32) and "… he who denies me before men will be denied before the angels of God" (Lk 12, 9).

"The kingdom of God is not coming with signs to be observed" (Lk 17, 20) and "… there will be signs in sun and moon and stars … And then they will see the Son of man coming ..." (Lk 21, 25, 27).

"All things are possible to him who believes" (Mk 9, 23) and "With men it is impossible ..." (Mk 10, 27).

"If your brother sins against you … and if he refuses to listen … let him be to you as a Gentile and a tax collector" (Matt. 18, 15-17) and "'how often shall my brother sin against me, and I forgive him?' … 'seventy times seven'" (Matt. 18, 21, 22).

"Do not swear at all" (Matt. 5, 34) and "So he who swears by the altar, swears by it and by everything on it" (Matt. 23, 20).

"Love your enemies" (Matt. 5, 44) and "woe to that man by whom the Son of man is betrayed! It would have been better for that man if he had not been born" (Matt. 26, 24).

"Do not lay up for yourselves treasures on earth" (Matt. 6, 19) and "to everyone who has will more be given" (Matt. 25, 29).

"I and the Father are one" (Jn 10, 30) and "I am the Son of God" (Jn 10, 36).

"the kingdom of God is in the midst of you" (Lk 17, 21) and "Then the righteous will shine ... in the kingdom of their Father" (Matt. 13, 43).

To "... to enter the kingdom of heaven ... he who does the will of my Father" (Matt. 7, 21) and "by your words you will be justified" (Matt. 12, 37).

"You ... must be perfect, as your heavenly Father is perfect" (Matt. 5, 48) and "No one is good but God alone" (Mk 10, 18).

"those who are accounted worthy to attain to ... the resurrection from the dead ... are equal to angels and are sons of God, being sons of the resurrection" (Lk 20, 35, 36) and "all who are in the tombs will ... come forth, those who have done good, to the resurrection of life, and those who have done evil, to the resurrection of judgement" (Jn 5, 28, 29).

"the gate is narrow ... that leads to life, and those who find it are few" (Matt. 7, 14) and "there will be two men ... one will be taken and the other left" (Lk 17, 34).

"you will not have gone through all the towns of Israel, before the Son of man comes" (Matt. 10, 23) and "this gospel ... will be preached throughout the whole world ... then the end will come" (Matt. 24, 14).

"Whatever you ask in my name, I will do it" (Jn 14, 13) and "If you abide in me, and my words abide in you, ask whatever you will, and it shall be done for you" (Jn 15, 7).

"offer for your cleansing what Moses commanded" (Mk 1, 44) and "'I desire mercy, and not sacrifice'" (Matt. 9, 13).

"Whoever ... relaxes one of the least of these commandments and teaches men so, shall be called least in the kingdom of heaven" (Matt. 5, 19) and "You have heard that it was said, 'An eye for an eye and a tooth for a tooth' ... But if anyone strikes you on the right cheek, turn to him the other also" (Matt. 5, 38, 39).

"Blessed are the peacemakers" (Matt. 5, 9) and "Do you think that I have come to give peace on earth? No, I tell you, but rather division" (Lk 12, 51).

"Beware of practising your piety before men in order to be seen by them" (Matt. 6, 1) and "when you are invited ... sit in the lowest place, so that ... your host ... may say to you, 'Friend, go up higher'; then you will be honoured in the presence of all ..." (Lk 14, 10).

Not strictly contradictory, but puzzling are, "I was sent only to the lost sheep of the house of Israel" (Matt. 15, 24) and "the kingdom of God will be taken away from you and given to a nation producing the fruits of it" (Matt. 21, 43). I estimate that in about half of these quotations the conflict could have been overcome by more explanation, such as Jesus clarifying that "to everyone who has will more be given" does not include material possessions; therefore, in about half of the examples the statements remain irreconcilable, such as "Judge not" and "judge". A contradiction between action and words arose when Jesus resisted the devil (Matt. 4, 1-11) and when he later decreed, "Do not resist one who is evil" (Matt. 5, 39).

In the gospels there are about forty references to "the scriptures" (Lk 24, 27), the Old Testament. When asked why he spoke in parables (Matt. 13, 10), Jesus drew on Isaiah chapter 6 verses 9 and 10 (Matt. 13, 14, 15. Com. Jeremiah 5, 21 and Ezekiel 12, 2). Isaiah was to tell the people not to understand lest they should take notice, repent and be forgiven. It is irony, by which he hopes to grab their attention, to "get through to them". In Matthew Jesus pointedly addresses the question why, but his answer is opaque; it could mean he speaks in parables because then the people do grasp the message, or then they do not, and if the latter he is suggesting that he does not want them to understand! It is the second interpretation that is implied by Mark and Luke, "... parables; so that they may ... not under-stand" (Mk 4, 11, 12; Lk 8, 9, 10). So it is Jesus' intention to obfuscate. He is, apparently, a sadist, holding forth, but deliberately obscurely, ensuring damnation. Unbelievable! Someone has made rather a hash of the original quotation. At 'the cleansing of the temple', Matthew and Luke record Jesus saying, "It is written, 'My house shall be... a house of prayer'" (Matt. 21, 13; Lk 19, 46; Isaiah 56, 7). Mark states the same, but he adds, "... for all the nations" (11, 17). Did he know that Jesus said these further words or did he himself insert them to complete the quotation ("... for all peoples," Isaiah 56, 7)? The words become an example of Jesus personally including Gentiles in his gospel, so they are important, but he may never have spoken them.

The Old Testament was also illustrated in some of the events in Jesus' life, and a few of these support the case for secondary additions in the gospels. In the story of "the triumphal entry" (Matt. 21, 1-11; Mk 11, 1-10;

Lk 19, 28-40; Jn 12, 12-16), Matthew and John quote from Zechariah chapter 9 verse 9, but Matthew places an "and" into the verse and, consequently, has Jesus instructing his disciples to bring an ass and a colt (21, 2) and he sits on both (21, 7)! Such was Matthew's adherence to what was written. Narrating the crucifixion, the synoptic gospels state that Jesus' garments were divided by the casting of lots (Matt. 27, 35: Mk 15, 24; Lk 23, 34). John states that the garments were split into four, "one for each soldier" (19, 23), but there was also a tunic, for which lots were cast (19, 24), and this was to fulfil the scripture, apparently psalm 22, 18, which mentions both "garments" and "raiment". Such was his adherence to what was written. Indeed, in describing the crucifixion he dwells very much on the scriptures: Jesus' words, "I thirst" were a fulfilment (19, 28), as was the need not to break any bones (19, 36), but he was "pierced" (19, 34), possibly to fulfil Zechariah 12, 10. These details are not given in the synoptic gospels. John seems to be jotting down as many passages as he can think of when he writes, "And again another scripture says ..." (19, 37). Did he weave some of what he presents as events around nothing other than old scriptural verses?

Jesus himself might have deliberately applied the Old Testament to his own life. He could have intended his "triumphal entry" to be a fulfilment of Zechariah chapter 9 verse 9. Miraculous interpretations apart, he planned it, according to Matthew, Mark and Luke without his disciples knowing (e.g. Mk 11, 2-6); likewise, his "last supper" (e.g. Mk 14, 12-16). Did he plan anything else? He foresaw in detail the end of his life (e.g. Mk 10, 33, 34). He anticipated being killed "and after three days" (Mk 10, 34. Com. Matt. 12, 40) or "on the third day" (Matt. 17, 23. Com. Lk 18, 33) he would rise, perhaps to fulfil Hosea chapter 6 verse 2. When the women (Matt. 28, 1; Mk 16, 1; Lk 24, 1) or Mary Magdalene (Jn 20, 1) arrived at his tomb they / she found an angel (Matt. 28, 2) or young man (Mk 16, 5) or two men, possibly angels (Lk 24, 4) or two angels (Jn 20, 12). If these beings were indeed men and not angels, what were they doing there? Did Jesus plan an apparent resurrection?

I find it presumptuous and perilous of the gospel writers or their sources to alter at all what they witnessed or received, especially to place words into the mouth of Jesus. The four writers themselves appear to have been believers. Matthew and Mark begin their narratives by calling Jesus "Christ" (Matt. 1, 1; Mk 1, 1) and Mark adds "the Son of God" (1, 1); Luke was at pains to tell "the truth" (Lk 1, 1-4) and he does not qualify his stories with phrases such as "it is said" - the miracles, for instance, are described as actual events. John blatantly wrote, "that you may believe that Jesus is the Christ, the Son of God" (20, 31). Surely they should have been fearful that to change, add to or take away from the testimony might incur the displeasure of their Lord. But it seems they were not afraid of this. I can only conclude they sincerely believed that their contributions were entirely acceptable to God. Considering the Old Testament they read of the prophets foretelling what would be done by and to the Messiah; Jesus was the Messiah; therefore what had been prophesied must have been done by or to him whether or not there was actual evidence of it. Presumably the gospel writers - John in particular - were also convinced they knew

Jesus' teaching well enough to amplify or amend it with his blessing.

The thrust of this section, The Pitfalls, has been to outline some of the problems in the gospels: the factual differences; the limitations of memory, necessitating editing; personal additions or subtractions, especially in John's gospel, and in the positioning of the "floating" verses, in the contents of the same discourse, in the appearance of themes, probably in Jesus' statements about Gentiles, and in the variations in the texts, indicating that writers were prepared to change the material; there are teachings inherently contradictory, and applying the Old Testament has caused occasional difficulties, with a few events seemingly based on it rather than on history. But - the great snag - I don't know which of the words attributed to Jesus were really spoken by him, so I will proceed as though all of them in the preferred text are authentic. Clearly, at times they point in different directions. So my criterion will be that Jesus' main teaching on any subject is that which is mainly taught; bearing in mind that that may amount to no more than a collection of similar points, the ones recalled and recorded, and they may not be the definitive teaching which itself may never have been formulated - but I can think of no better touchstone.

Theology

God

"God is spirit" (Jn 4, 24) personified, seeing (Matt. 6, 6) and knowing (Matt. 6, 8). Jesus commonly refers to God as "Father" (e.g. "Our Father ...", Matt. 6, 9) and always as "he". Men speak to him through prayer. He resides "in heaven" (Matt. 6, 9) which seems to be in the sky (Lk 17, 29; 10, 18; Jn 6, 38).

Named "The Lord" (e.g. Mk 12, 29), he is "the only God" (Jn 5, 44. See, also, Jn 17, 3; Mk 12, 32, 34). He is "perfect" (Matt. 5, 48) and with him "all things are possible" (Matt. 19, 26). One might ask how he can square circles? Perhaps Jesus wasn't mindful of any such conundrum. It was a statement of omnipotence.

God began the creation (Mk 13, 19) and he provides for life on earth, feeding the birds (Matt. 6, 26), clothing the grass (Matt. 6, 30), so don't be "anxious" (Matt. 6, 31) about food or drink or clothes. Unfortunately, of course, many people have to be extremely anxious about these essentials. "... seek first his kingdom and his righteousness" (Matt. 6, 33). That is the priority. "... love the Lord your God" (Mk 12, 30) wholeheartedly. His "will be done" (Matt. 6, 10).

Jesus

Jesus indicated that he was a prophet (Mk 6, 4; Lk 13, 33) and he certainly spoke like one declaring "the words which thou (God) gavest me" (Jn 17, 8), and predicting the future (e.g. Mk 13, 1-27). He called himself "The Teacher" (Lk 22, 11), "the Son of man" (Jn 9, 35 -37), "Christ" (Jn 4, 25, 26), "Lord" (Jn 13, 13) and "the Son of God" (Jn 10, 36).

On occasions he implied, strictly, that he himself was God - "He who has seen me has seen the Father" (Jn 14, 9) and "I and the Father are one" (Jn 10, 30), though when challenged on the second statement he referred to scripture as meaning those to whom the word came could be called "gods" (Jn 10, 34, 35. See Psalm 82, 6); then he reverted to calling himself "the Son of God" (Jn 10, 36) which, overwhelmingly, was his usual description of the relationship. Almost always Jesus drew a distinction between God and himself. God was his father. He prayed to God. He spoke as God had "bidden" him (Jn 12, 50). Only the Father knew the time of Jesus' second coming (Mk 13, 32) and he decided who would sit either side of his son (Matt. 20, 23). "I go to the Father," Jesus said. "... the Father is greater than I" (Jn 14, 28. Com. Jn 13, 16).

The "oneness" of God and son was extended to others. Jesus prayed that believers - not only the disciples - "may be one even as we (God and Jesus) are one" (Jn 17, 22). He said, "the Father is in me and I am in the Father" (Jn 10, 38) and sought that believers "also may be in us" (Jn 17, 21). What he did not say was that they should all coalesce into one mass. He was separate from his Father, his believers were from each other and they would continue to be - in the new kingdom he would sit "at the right hand of the power of God" (Lk 22, 69) and his disciples "on thrones" (Lk 22, 30) - notice the plural, "thrones". They were not to be one in a literal sense but in terms of nature, values, standards and purpose. Today we use the expression, "of one mind". These immaterial essences were inside God and himself and, he hoped, they would be inside his believers, uniting all. To see Jesus was not to see the actual entity but the personality of God.

Again, today we say that we "see" characteristics of one person in another. Describing, though, not the characteristics but the characters themselves as being one or inside of one another was arresting, dramatic. It emphasised their closeness to each other and, as such, served to boost affection and resolution. Sometimes Jesus' words were puzzling and needed unravelling (e.g. Jn 4, 31-33). No doubt it was with some relief that his disciples exclaimed, "Ah, now you are speaking plainly, not in any figure!" (Jn 16, 29).

If Jesus was not God himself, one unique trait he suggested he shared with God was pre-existence: he existed before his life on earth, indeed, before the world began. He wished that his disciples would behold the glory he had been given "before the foundation of the world" (Jn 17, 24). Should this be interpreted as meaning that God, foreseeing the future, gave glory to an as yet non-existent Jesus, then a stronger verse is John chapter 17 verse 5, "Father, glorify thou me …with the glory which I had with thee before the world was made". Here it would be stretching exegesis to claim that Jesus was no more than a thought. He appears as a person - "I" - whose glory was personally experienced before the creation. In an argument the "Jews" ask Jesus if he is saying that he has seen Abraham (Jn 8, 57). He replies, "before Abraham was, I am" (Jn 8, 58). Assuming "I am" is not to be understood as the name for God (see Exodus 3, 13, 14), and it doesn't seem to have been, Jesus is apparently saying that he existed before Abraham who, chronologically, preceded him by about two thousand years. A clear indication of Jesus' pre-existence comes in his response to his disciples finding some of his teaching difficult, "Do you take offence at this? Then what if you were to see the Son of man ascending where he was before?" (Jn 6, 61, 62. com. Jn 3, 13; 6, 38, 51; 7,29; 16, 28).

A personage Jesus denied being, in one teaching, was "The son of David" (Matt. 22, 42); to be precise, a descendant since King David lived some thousand years before him. He reasons how can it be said that the Christ is David's son when David himself addresses the Christ as "Lord" (Matt. 22, 43-45. Psalm 110, 1)? Taking Jesus to be the Christ, his Old Testament interpretation provides more evidence of his pre-existence, but his rejection that he was a "son" of David was unusual and could be detrimental. When he was addressed as such, and repeatedly (Mk 10, 46-48), he did not repudiate the title (Mk 10, 49-52), nor when he was called it by the Canaanite woman (Matt. 15, 22), and he readily accepted the crowds shouting it during his "triumphal entry" (Matt. 21, 9, 15, 16). The genealogies in Matthew (1, 1-16) and Luke (3, 23-38) both trace Jesus through the line of David, and this helped. The idea that the Christ was a Davidic descendant was certainly well-known (e.g. 2 Samuel 7, 16; Jeremiah 33, 14-16; Ezekiel 34, 23, 24), and its belief was probably widespread (e.g. Lk 1, 32, 69; Matt. 12, 23; 21, 9; Jn 7, 42). In arguing that this was not true Jesus could have done more harm than good, and quite unnecessarily; he raised the topic, it was not thrust upon him. Was he trying to outdo the religious leaders who had been trying so hard to outdo him (Matt. 22, 15-46)? If so, perhaps this particular victory was short-sighted.

God sent Jesus to "preach the good news" (Lk 4, 43). He "came... to call … sinners" (Matt. 9, 13), "to seek and to save the lost" (Lk 19, 20). They were to "repent, and believe in the gospel" (Mk 1, 15). The righteous would earn "eternal life" (Matt. 25, 46) "in the kingdom of their Father" (Matt. 13, 43) which was "at hand" (Mk 1, 15). "The time" was "fulfilled" (Mk 1, 15).

Jesus spoke of himself as a servant (Lk 22, 27; Matt. 20, 28); he also spoke of himself as a king (Jn 4, 25, 26. Com. Lk 23, 2). It may be said that kings serve by performing their duty. Jesus' service was to entreat people to repent and reform and so gain a blissful life after death. He advocated humility - and an unflamboyant (Matt. 6,1) and unmaterialistic (Matt. 6,19) lifestyle - but in his stance he was always authoritative. Blunt with even the rulers of his day (e.g. Lk 11, 39, 46; Jn 18, 20, 21; 19, 11), he didn't mince his words with anyone. He was "master" (Matt. 23, 10)and he reminded his disciples of this on the occasion that he acted very much like a servant - "... I... your Lord and Teacher, have washed your feet ..." (Jn 13, 14). He was a mixture of server and instructor; at his second coming he would be manifestly a king.

Jesus served, apparently to the point of giving "his life as a ransom for many" (Matt. 20, 28). At "the last supper" he compared the bread to his body and the wine to his blood "... which is poured out for many for the forgiveness of sins" (Matt. 26, 28). He might mean he hoped his martyrdom would inspire others to change their ways (Jn 12, 32) and so be forgiven, or maybe, that it would demonstrate his extreme concern for men and soften God's appraisal of, and response to, them (com. Numbers 14, 10-23). But the words suggest he is a sacrifice in the traditional sense of taking upon himself the sins of others (e.g. Leviticus 16, 21, 22) and, as noted, this concept can be no more than symbolic because his predominant teaching is that men's sins are removed by their own genuine repentance and determination to do better. Jesus would be contradicting these principles if he took away people's sins without them doing anything. The sinner must personally enable the removal of his sins.

As the Christ, Jesus had been "written about" (Lk 24, 44. Com. Jn 5, 46; Lk 18, 31) in The Old Testament. It was "necessary that the Christ should suffer" (Lk 24, 26), and so he predicted - he would "be delivered to the chief priests …, and they will condemn him to death, and deliver him to the Gentiles; and they will mock him, and spit upon him, and scourge him, and kill him" (Mk 10, 33, 34), but "after three days he will rise" (Mk 10, 34). Though "going to the Father" (Jn 16,28), sometime he would return to the earth "on the clouds of heaven with power and great glory" (Matt. 24, 30), "the King" (Matt. 25, 34) seated "on his glorious throne" (Matt. 25, 31),establishing "his kingdom" (Matt. 16, 28), "the new world" (Matt. 19, 28), seemingly forever (Matt. 19, 29).

The Holy Spirit

Spirit suggests something intangible, and so the Holy Spirit seems to be. Jesus "breathed on" the disciples, "and said to them, 'Receive the Holy Spirit'" (Jn 20, 22). It supplies inspiration (Mk 12, 36), spontaneous speech (Mk 13, 11) and, perhaps, "power" (Lk 24, 49. Com. Acts 2, 1-4). God will "give" it "to those who ask him" (Lk 11, 13). Jesus described it as "the Counsellor" who would "bring to your remembrance all that I have said to you" (Jn 14, 26). "He", the counsellor, was "the Spirit of truth" (Jn 15, 26) who would "guide you into all the truth" (Jn 16, 13).

The Holy Spirit is distinct from the Father and the Son (Matt. 28, 19), but, as with them, there is an extremely close connection. It "proceeds from the Father" (Jn 15, 26) who will "send" it in the name of the Son (Jn 14, 26). It appears to be meant by "the Spirit of your Father" (Matt. 10, 20; comparing Matt. 10, 19, 20 with Mk 13, 11 and Lk 12, 11, 12) which is surely the same as "the spirit of God" (Matt. 12, 28. Com. Matt. 12, 31, 32). "... the Spirit ... will not speak on his own authority, but whatever he hears he will speak" (Jn 16, 13), presumably whatever he hears from God and from Jesus who himself spoke the words of God (Jn 17, 8). Both Jesus and the Holy Spirit will tell the disciples what to say in their hour of need (Mk 13, 11; Lk 21, 14, 15). God, Jesus and the Holy Spirit seem to be as one in thought and speech.

"... every sin and blasphemy will be forgiven men, but the blasphemy against the Spirit will not be forgiven. And whoever says a word against the Son of man will be forgiven; but whoever speaks against the Holy Spirit will not be forgiven, either in this age or in the age to come" (Matt. 12, 31, 32) - such speech is "an eternal sin" (Mk 3, 29). So, to speak against Jesus will be forgiven, but to speak against the Holy Spirit will not be, ever. Yet in the very verse which precedes Luke's version of this quotation (Lk 12, 9), Jesus says that whoever denies him will themselves be denied, so in this case they too are not forgiven, though he does not add "ever". And given the intensely inter-woven natures of God, Jesus and the Holy Spirit impugning one would inevitably entail impugning all three, with, seemingly, the same fateful consequence.

What, precisely, amounts to "speaking against"? Jesus' words about criticism of himself and the Holy Spirit (Matt. 12, 31, 32) come within a story where the

Pharisees state he performs miracles by the power of the devil (Matt. 12, 24). I can well imagine him taking offence at that accusation. What, though, of sincere, serious consideration, which is only natural but which may lead to puzzlement and doubt? I have raised the logical perplexity of squaring circles. Many people grapple with occurrences of natural disasters and barbaric acts, especially those involving the deaths of the innocent, such as young children. Why does God permit them? Is probing these problems "speaking against" because one is querying the nature of God, wondering if he is as perfect as he is meant to be? Yet, given the world as we find it, such questions are only to be expected; for the believer they are answered by faith - he doesn't know the solutions but he trusts that God does. Perhaps, then, it is definite criticism that is condemned. It is not difficult to recognise many cases where the line has been crossed, but it is not clear just where the line is.

The Kingdom of God

Though it makes clear that the entire universe is God's kingdom (Genesis 1, 1), the Bible concentrates on one particular part, inhabited by God and the righteous (e.g. Lk 13, 28). It is also called heaven (com. Lk 13, 28 to Matt. 8, 11).

Jesus began his preaching by pronouncing that "the kingdom of God" (Mk 1, 15) or "... heaven" (Matt. 4, 17) "is at hand" (Matt. 4, 17; Mk 1, 15), about to arrive (Mk 9, 1; Lk 21, 31, 32). During his ministry he told the Pharisees that the kingdom of God had "come upon" them (Matt. 12, 28), it was "in the midst of" them (Lk 17, 21), and in their evangelising his disciples were to declare it had "come near" (Lk 10, 9). It seems, then, that it appeared or approached during Jesus' earthly life, but in what sense - not in the normal one of a significant spatial area? The first reference (Matt. 12, 28), in full, implies that the presence of the kingdom is shown by God enabling Jesus to perform miracles; the second (Lk 17, 21) leaves me wondering just what is meant by the word "kingdom" with possibilities ranging from Jesus himself to an inner, spiritual component, and the third (Lk 10, 9) suggests that the kingdom has been indicated by miracles and messengers. In each case what seems to be really referred to are people, power and spirituality. Onlookers were glimpsing not a domain but characters and characteristics of the kingdom of God. Striving to give these verses a territorial sense, implicit in the word "kingdom", one could say it is not just in one place, but also wherever a believer is. He exemplifies it, and where he stands is a physical fraction of it.

Continuing this idea, the kingdom expands as the number of believers increases. Whether or not Jesus had this, precisely, in mind, he certainly spoke of the kingdom growing: he compared it to seed becoming grain (Mk 4, 26 - 29), to a mustard seed, "the smallest of all", swelling into "the greatest of all shrubs" (Mk 4, 30 - 32) and to leaven placed in meal "till it was all leavened" (Lk 13, 20, 21). Yet, despite the last illustration, the kingdom will not grow until it embraces everyone. There will always be those who reject or disobey it. Eventually it, the actual territory, will be imposed, replacing all others, the one, sovereign kingdom. According to the parable of The Wheat and the Weeds (Matt. 13, 24 - 30) Jesus "will send his angels, and they will gather out of his kingdom all causes of sin and all evildoers ... Then the righteous will shine like the sun in the kingdom of their Father" (Matt. 13, 41, 43). The parousia passages in Matthew and Mark write of the angels gathering not sinners, but the elect (Matt. 24, 31; Mk 13, 27); each synoptic gospel writes of Jesus himself "coming" (Matt. 24, 30; Mk 13, 26; Lk 21, 27), Matthew of him sitting "on his glorious throne" (Matt. 25, 31) and separating the good from the bad (Matt. 25, 31 - 46).

The good will live in the kingdom which may continue to be where it is, in heaven, and the righteous taken there (Jn 14, 2, 3); but the removal of "all causes of sin and all evildoers" (Matt. 13, 41) implies a cleansed world, a "new world" (Matt 19, 28) and the kingdom, or a part of it, may relocate to earth. "I saw a new heaven and a new earth ... I saw the holy city, new Jerusalem, coming down out of heaven ..." (The Revelation to John 21, 1, 2).

Salvation

Who is to enter the kingdom of God? Who is to be saved? The righteous, but what makes them so? Two general criteria are, "he who does the will of my Father" (Matt. 7, 21) and "… whoever believes in him" (i.e. Jesus) (Jn 3, 15). There are verses that imply that one particular attribute will on its own provide admission - forgiving (Matt. 6, 14), not judging (Matt. 7, 1), speaking carefully (Matt. 12, 36, 37), being poor (Lk 6, 20), being persecuted (Lk 6, 22, 23) and hating one's "life in this world" (Jn 12, 25). Some parables call for specific practices: forgiveness (The Unmerciful Servant, Matt. 18, 23-35), helpfulness (The Good Samaritan, Lk 10, 30-37), faithfulness (The Faithful Steward, Lk 12, 42-44) and productiveness (The Talents, Matt. 25, 14 -30). A person, though, could radiate one of these qualities whilst sinning in many other ways. Someone could forgive but speak carelessly; be poor but judgemental. Then he is accepted for the one, but rejected for the other. So wouldn't he really be judged overall? The safest course is surely to be mindful of all of the precepts.

To "enter life" Jesus tells a man to "keep the commandments" (Matt. 19, 17) and he lists some, mostly from the ten commandments, whilst in reply to a similar question from a lawyer he affirms the lawyer's own answer, "love the Lord … and your neighbour …" (Lk 10, 25-28); the first is, "the great commandment" (Matt. 22, 38) and the second "is like it" (Matt. 22, 39).

If by saying one must "receive the kingdom of God like a child" (Mk 10, 15), Jesus means on trust then anyone who has reasoned their way to God is excluded. "… unless one is born of water …" (Jn 3, 5) strongly suggests that baptism, a ritual, is necessary for salvation. What of a believer who through no fault of his own has not been baptised, "the penitent thief" (Lk 23, 39-43) for instance? Jesus told him, "… today you will be with me in Paradise" (Lk 23, 43).

Many stipulations and some difficulties! Assuming Jesus spoke extemporaneously, on numerous occasions, in different situations and, perhaps, over a few years, it is not surprising that the collection of his statements that we possess do not always knit together. Frequently when speaking our vocabulary is imprecise, our sentences lack qualifications, not taking sufficient account of other factors; in making a point we may over-stress its importance and if we make a few points one may be at some variance with another. When Jesus said, "… by your words you will be justified, and by your words you will be condemned" (Matt. 12, 37) he was speaking in a context of words - he had just been accused of consorting with the devil (Matt. 12, 24). His response overstated the literal case; words are not the be all and end all; he had already implied that entry to the kingdom was gained by deeds (Matt, 7, 21); and, reason decrees, the actual position is that entry is gained by striving to fulfil a variety of conditions and, I venture, there will also be a consideration of circumstances. Justice demands no less. The gospels are not painstakingly argued conclusions - which may nonetheless contain errors - but recollections of Jesus' life and teaching, which reminds us that inconsistencies may come not from Jesus but from those telling and recording memories and possibly adding their own views - I think again of how differently Matthew and Luke recount the beatitudes (Matt. 5, 3 - 12; Lk 6, 20 -23). We are left to try and find the fundamental threads.

Concerning salvation, I propose that Jesus basically taught, honour God and himself and obey their commands as revealed in the Bible. It will not suffice to disbelieve in or disregard Deity and Son but to lead a good life morally - you must "love the Lord your God" (Mk 12, 30); it will not suffice to believe in them but to lead a bad life morally - you must "love your neighbour" (Mk 12, 31), and love must be shown in action.

What cannot be expected, though, is that a person will always obey all of the commands. Jesus told his hearers that they "must be perfect" (Matt. 5, 48), like God, but he told the rich man that "No one is good but God alone" (Mk 10, 18). He spoke of "righteous persons who need no repentance" (Lk 15, 7), but the Lord's prayer includes "forgive us our sins" (Lk 11, 4), as though sins are inevitable (com. Matt. 7, 11; Lk 13, 3; 18, 9–14), and since thoughts as well as deeds are counted (Mk 7, 21; Matt. 5, 27, 28) who does not - cannot - sin? Jesus implied that in general sins are forgiven (Matt. 12, 31. Com. Matt. 6, 14), but not regardless for that would mean no matter what a person says or does he would still be saved. Then what is the point of God's and Jesus' commands, of judgement, of hell, of Jesus' mission? The message would be whatever you do you will go to heaven. Clearly that is not what the gospels say. For forgiveness a person must repent. Believers are expected to follow the rules, but sometimes they will fail; then they should be sorry and strive to do better, and, with some exceptions (e.g. Matt. 12, 31b; 18, 6; 26, 24), they will be forgiven. Jesus came "to call … sinners to repentance" (Lk 5, 32. Com. Matt. 4, 17; Mk 1, 15; Jn 8, 24). The choice was "repent" or "perish" (Lk 13, 5) as Chorazin, Bethsaida, Capernaum and "this generation" would discover to their cost (Matt. 11, 21-24; 12, 41, 42).

Jesus compared sinners to "the lost" (Lk 19, 10; 15) and when they are "found" (Lk 15, 5, 9), to be precise, find themselves ("… came to himself", Lk 15, 17), that is, when they repent, there is "joy in heaven" (Lk 15, 7). The disciples were to preach "repentance and forgiveness of sins" (Lk 24, 47). They personally were empowered to "forgive" or "retain" anyone's sins (Jn 20, 23).

I take it for granted that God would not accept false repentance, someone who didn't mean it or who deliberately sinned intending to nullify it with an apology. Indeed, someone who spent much of their life sinning assuming they would nonetheless be saved if they managed "sorry" with their dying breath, would, I infer, have "deceit" (Mk 7, 22) added to their wrongdoings. Real repentance implies genuine sorrow and a determination to try to live righteously; compensation, if possible, is fitting, as in the story of Zacchaeus (Lk 19, 1-10). "Bear fruit that befits repentance" (Matt. 3, 8) declared John the Baptist.

Resurrection

To prove "that the dead are raised" (Lk 20, 37) Jesus refers to the Lord being the God of Abraham, Isaac and Jacob and he is God of the living. The reasoning seems to be that since these famous men of the Old Testament died (Genesis 25, 8; 35, 29; 49, 33), and the Lord is their god and he is god of the living, then they are alive, so they must have been raised from the dead. Further, "... those who are accounted worthy to attain to ... the resurrection from the dead ... are equal to angels and are sons of God, being sons of the resurrection" (Lk 20, 35, 36. Com. Lk 14,14, "the resurrection of the just"; also, Matt. 22, 30; Mk 12, 25). Evidently, they are good people.

Here there is no mention of the resurrection of bad people. The implication is that only the good are raised.

Then, "... the hour is coming when all who are in the tombs will hear his voice and come forth, those who have done good, to the resurrection of life, and those who have done evil, to the resurrection of judgement" (Jn 5, 28, 29). A very definite statement that good and bad are raised! This view is also expressed through the story of the rich man and Lazarus (Lk 16, 19-31); both die, the rich man goes to "Hades" and "torment" (v. 23), Lazarus to "Abraham's bosom" (v. 22) - one to hell, one to heaven.

Though I find them inconclusive, there are phrases too that could support the resurrection of both the righteous and the unrighteous: Jesus ends his treatment of the subject with "... for all live to him" (Lk 20, 38) which might mean everyone is raised, though he has just implied that they are not, and despite "for" the phrase is not a deduction but an addition which might be a few concluding words of devotion such as, all live to his glory; again, "The men of Nineveh will arise at the judgement with this generation and condemn it" (Lk 11, 32). Presumably "the men" will include some who are bad. The whole sentence may be dramatic licence, but taking it literally Jesus is speaking collectively and in that sense he goes on to say "they repented" (Lk 11, 32), so they should be saved. Thirdly, Jesus "will repay every man for what he has done" (Matt. 16, 27); if he means every person who has ever lived then, of course, an enormous number of all types would have to be brought back to life, but he might mean everyone who is alive at the time of his second coming. Certainly when he returns the living, good and bad, will be repaid. The parousia passages themselves shed no light on the matter; they tell merely of the angels gathering "his elect" (Matt. 24, 31; Mk 13, 27); there is no mention of anybody being raised, but their reference to the elect suggests if anybody is, it will be the good.

The good will rise to "life", the evil to "judgement" (Jn 5, 29). In the gospels when Jesus speaks of life meaning the existence to come he seems to mean exclusively in heaven. The righteous are awarded "life" (e.g. Matt. 25, 46; Mk 9, 43; Lk 9, 24; Jn 5, 39, 40). Bearing this in mind, very near John chapter 5 verses 28, 29, the good and the bad, Jesus declares, "... the Father raises the dead and gives them life ..." (Jn 5, 21), and in words similar to John chapter 5 verse 28, "... the hour is coming, and now is, when the dead will hear the voice of the Son of God, and those who hear will live" (Jn 5, 25). So even in John's gospel and around the very spot where he declares resurrection for all, Jesus strongly suggests resurrection for the righteous only (see, also, Jn 6, 39, 40, 44, 54). There is indeed the prospect that they themselves are not raised - do not need to be - because they "will never see death" (Jn 8, 51), an apparent overstatement of "he who ... believes ... has passed from death to life" (Jn 5, 24).

It may be proposed that Jesus' emphasis on the raising of the good was only a part of the teaching, perhaps to stress the reward of goodness; if asked, he would have asserted that the bad are raised too. But when he addressed the subject specifically (Lk 20, 34-38) he clearly implied that only the righteous are resurrected; if he really held that wrongdoers are as well surely he would not have expressed himself as he did, he would have taught their inclusion more often and not so often have given the contrary impression. In his comparison with the days of Noah and Lot (Lk 17, 26-30) Jesus made it very clear that the bad who are alive when he returns will be punished. What of the bad who are dead?

It may be reasoned it is only just that the unrighteous who have died should suffer the same fate as those who are alive on the day of judgement. God would insist upon it. A sound point, I think, but not one that Jesus himself laid down, and there are places where he indicates the entire punishment for the unrighteous is to be denied entry to the kingdom of God (e.g. Matt. 25, 1-12; Lk 13, 25-28; 17, 34, 35. Possibly also, Matt. 24, 31; Mk 13, 27) which of course would apply to those who were not resurrected. Should the bad go to hell that would be a reason for raising the ones who have died otherwise they would escape that outcome. All very fair, but not actually argued in the gospels.

Jesus definitely taught that good people are raised from the dead; whether bad people are too is uncertain - most of his statements favour the resurrection of only the good.

When are those concerned raised? When they "hear the voice of the Son of God" (Jn 5, 25), "at the last day" (Jn 6, 40); that "hour is coming, and now is" (Jn 5, 25); it is "that age" (Lk 20, 35), the age of "the resurrection from the dead" (Lk 20, 35). Yet, in the course of saying this Jesus also implies that Abraham, Isaac and Jacob are alive at present (Lk 20, 37, 38). Perhaps he was considering death as dormant life - the patriarchs are indeed dead, but for them this state is transitory, they are just waiting to be raised. Jesus referred to Jairus' daughter and to Lazarus as asleep (Mk 5, 39; Jn 11, 11) though he knew as well as anyone that they were dead. But they could be brought back from the dead. It was like waking them up. They were potentially alive. In Luke chapter 20 verses 37 and 38, however, Jesus is meeting the challenge of the dead being raised head - on, and there is no hint that "dead" and "living" (Lk 20, 38) mean anything other than the normal meaning of those words. The Lord is the God of the three patriarchs now and "he is not God of the dead, but of the living" (Lk 20, 38), so they must be alive now. If Jesus was thinking figuratively I would like to see some sign of it within these verses. It seems to me when one really wants to make a point, one makes it very plainly, no room for doubt, the words are to be taken literally.

Moreover, Abraham, Isaac and Jacob were not the only ones restored to life before the day of judgement. It is not teaching, true, but we are told that during the transfiguration (Mk 9, 2 - 8) Jesus talked with Elijah and Moses (9, 4). According to the Old Testament, Elijah never died (2 Kings 2, 11) but Moses did (Deuteronomy 34, 5), so he would have to be raised. Then, of course, there is Jesus himself - he predicted his own resurrection to happen shortly after his death (e.g. Mk 10, 33, 34), whilst his words to the penitent thief (Lk 23, 43) necessitate both him and the thief being raised on the day they died. In his narration of the rich man and Lazarus (Lk 16, 19-31) Jesus has the two men dying and being brought to life shortly afterwards, and he does not indicate that this was at all exceptional. There are, then, specific examples of people who have been resurrected before any particular day of resurrection, and perhaps others have been too (Lk 20, 38; 16, 22, 23, extended to people in general).

The story of the rich man and Lazarus also prompts the concept of the soul, an immaterial embodiment of self. The rich man was both "buried" (Lk 16, 22) and "in Hades" (16, 23). He cannot be in two places at once; the solution may be that he was in two forms - the body in the grave, the soul in Hades. In the parable of The Rich Fool, God tells that rich man, "This night your soul is required of you" (Lk 12, 20). He will die and his soul will be claimed. Jesus pronounced love God "with all your soul" (Mk 12, 30), and it is distinguished from heart, mind and strength (Mk 12, 30), whilst in telling his disciples what to fear (Matt. 10, 28) Jesus separates the soul, which seems to survive death, from the body, which for the time being at least seems to perish with death. So, a person does have a soul, and the word is presented as usually understood.

Another concept to be considered is, spirit. In saying, "the spirit indeed is willing ..." (Matt. 26, 41) Jesus may be referring to the wish, the will, the enthusiasm, but when he tried to assure the disciples that he was not "a spirit" (Lk 24, 39) he stated and demonstrated differences between a human and an apparition (Lk 24, 39-43). On the occasion that his disciples saw him walking on the water and thought he was "a ghost" (Mk 6, 49) his response was, "Take heart, it is I" (6, 50) -again, he was not a ghost. Clearly, though, he and his disciples were at least acquainted with the notion. Spirit can also mean soul, as in, "Father, into thy hands I commit my spirit!" (Lk 23, 46).

How often have we spoken of ghosts whether or not we think they exist? I do not conclude that Jesus' assertions that he was not one indicate that he believed in them, though I am rather surprised that given the nature of his teaching, the appropriateness of a repudiation of all ghosts when his followers feared he was one and his painstaking methods to prove he was not (Lk 24, 39-43), he didn't mention anywhere along the way that really there aren't any! In speaking of the soul, however, Jesus does indeed state that it exists and indicates that it is individual and eternal (Matt. 10, 28; Mk 12, 30; Lk 12, 4, 5; 12, 20; 16, 22-26; 23, 46). So what happens to it when a person dies? Reasonably, it should be judged and enter the after-life at that point, as in the story of the rich man and Lazarus (Lk 16, 19-31), for why should it remain imprisoned, as it were, inside a corpse until a certain day? And if it does move on as proposed, there is no need for a general resurrection and the day of judgement would apply only to those who were alive at the time.

The gospels contain verses declaring one collective resurrection and verses suggesting that everyone continues to exist when they die. There are souls and spirits and presumed ghosts. We are left with two different prospects, dead until a particular time and, secondly, die in body, live in spirit; the first is explicitly taught and so gains the priority; the second emerges almost unnoticed, but it is there, seemingly more than Jesus himself recognised.

The Day of Judgement

This is the day when Jesus reveals which people are good and which bad, who is to be rewarded, who punished. According to the parousia sections (Matt. 24; Mk 13; Lk 21, 5-36) it will be preceded by catastrophes - false Christs leading many astray, wars, famines, earthquakes, persecutions, the conquest and defilement of Jerusalem and the malfunctioning of the sun, moon and stars. Despite the statement that there will not be signs (Lk 17, 20, 21), these are the signs (Lk 21, 11, 25) that the kingdom of God is about to be established. Following the cosmic turbulence Jesus will come "in clouds with great power and glory. And then he will send out the angels, and gather his elect" (Mk 13, 26, 27). The parable of The Wheat and the Weeds (Matt. 13, 24-30, 37-43) has the angels plucking out all evildoers (Matt. 13, 41), whilst in the story of the sheep and the goats Jesus says he himself will judge the nations which will be gathered before him (Matt. 25, 31, 32). His disciples will judge Israel (Matt. 19, 28; Lk 22, 30). Believers at least will be raised from the dead on this day (Jn 6, 40). In places Jesus signifies that the number of people who are saved will be "few" (e.g. Matt. 7, 13, 14), perhaps even in single figures! He compares them to Noah and his family (Lk 17, 26, 27) - eight altogether (Genesis 6, 10; 7, 7) and to Lot and his family (Lk 17, 28-30) - four altogether (Genesis 19, 15, 16). Everyone else will be "destroyed" (Lk 17, 27, 29). However, following the comparisons he suggests more of a fifty-fifty outcome, "one will be taken and the other left" (Lk 17, 34, 35. Com. Matt. 25, 1-13).

Exactly when Jesus will come only God knows (Matt. 24, 36), but it would be within the lifetime of his own generation (Matt. 16, 28; 24, 34; Mk 9, 1; 13, 30; Lk 9, 27; 21, 32. Also, Matt. 4, 17; 24, 33, "you" - his hearers; Mk 1, 15; 13, 29; Lk 12, 40; 18, 7, 8a; 21, 28, 31; Jn 5, 25, "now is"; 21, 22, 23). First, "this gospel ... will be preached throughout the whole world" (Matt 24, 14). For this to be achieved within about forty years - the span of his own generation - may appear over-ambitious, but perhaps this was Jesus' expectation. He may have envisaged the world as smaller than we know it to be. Matthew chapter 10 verse 23 could mean the gospel will not even have been preached throughout Israel let alone the world before Jesus returns, in glory. What if, on that day, there are individuals who have never heard it? What will happen to them? Luke chapter 12 verses 47 and 48 point to people being treated according to what they knew, and surely this is only right. So a person who did not know of the gospel cannot be punished for not accepting or observing it. He might be censored or commended according to the standards he did know. The context of these verses is the story of the faithful and the unfaithful steward

(Lk 12, 42-46): the first is rewarded because he performed his duty; the second is punished because he misused his responsibility. The role of duty is recognised world-wide. But, of course, Jesus' teaching comprises much more than particular duty - many additional moral injunctions and essential theological beliefs. It is unclear how someone who is unaware of Christianity will be judged. Perhaps it is assumed that everyone will be aware of it (Matt. 24, 14). The patriarchs and prophets - and maybe others - who lived before Jesus and who are in the kingdom of God (Lk 13, 28) presumably gained their places exceptionally. What is clear is that anyone who has received the gospel must embrace it if they are to be saved (Jn 8, 24; 15, 4 -6; Lk 13, 5); anyone who ignores or rejects it will themselves be rejected (Matt. 10, 14, 32, 33; Mk 8, 38).

Reward

The reward for the righteous is to be admitted to heaven, the home of God (Matt. 5, 34; 6, 9). Jesus said very little about the nature of heaven. He did not mention perpetual adoration of God (see Revelation 4), lush landscapes, a balmy climate or, indeed, wings except in connection with "a hen" (Matt. 23, 37). Taking "my Father's house" to mean heaven, he did say it contains "many rooms" (Jn 14, 2), and there "neither moth nor rust consumes and … thieves do not break in and steal" (Matt. 6, 20).

God rules (Matt. 5, 34) with Jesus at his right hand (Lk 22, 69). There are "those for whom" sitting either side of Jesus "has been prepared" (Matt. 20, 23) and, of course, the disciples are there (Lk 22, 28-30). Favoured also are the "poor" (Lk 6, 20), "the poor in spirit" (Matt.

5, 3) and the persecuted (Matt. 5, 11, 12). In the kingdom "the righteous will shine like the sun" (Matt. 13, 43), they "are like angels" (Mk 12, 25), living forever (Matt. 25, 46; Mk 10, 30; Jn 10, 27,28), no doubt happily.

Punishment

The unrighteous are not allowed into heaven. Jesus taught that they are "left" (Matt. 24, 40,41), shut out (Matt. 25, 1-12; Lk 13, 28), "destroyed" (Lk 17, 27, 29. See, also, Matt. 22, 7; Mk 12, 9; Lk 19, 27), thrown "into the outer darkness" (Matt. 8, 12; 22, 13; 25, 30) and thrown "into the furnace of fire" (Matt. 13, 50. See, also, Mk 9, 43; Lk 16, 24; Jn 15, 6). The place of the fire is called hell (Mk 9, 43), "prepared for the devil and his angels" (Matt. 25, 41) and, evidently, for the unrighteous, the "cursed" (Matt. 25, 41). The fire is "unquenchable" (Mk 9, 43). Whatever the exact punishment, it seems to be "eternal" (Matt. 25, 46; Mk 3, 29; 9, 48. Possibly Lk 16, 9), though Jesus referring to imprisonment until a debt has been repaid (Matt. 5, 26; 18, 34) offers, theoretically at least, a chance of expiation whilst serving the penalty. Matthew chapter 18 verse 35 implies that God will do as the king did, that is, make the sentence conditional.

But perhaps the parallel should not be pressed to this point. Jesus may have been emphasising only that God will be as angry as the king at such behaviour and will punish the miscreant. Other quotations cited contain no hint of post-judgement redemption and forgiveness. Mark chapter 9 verse 48 covers sin generally and implies eternity. Two particular sins that incur everlasting punishment are blaspheming the Holy Spirit (Mk 3, 29) and ignoring the needy (Matt. 25, 46); as discussed, though, disrespect of the Holy Spirit includes disrespect of God and Jesus; and if not assisting those in need is so egregious surely there are a multitude of transgressions which should be similarly assessed. The particular, then, broadens into the general. In the story of the rich man and Lazarus (Lk 16, 19-31) we are told there is no crossing between heaven and hell for "a great chasm has been fixed, in order that those who would pass from here to you may not be able, and none may cross from there to us" (Lk 16, 26).

Concluding, then, that the punishment is eternal, there is symmetry between an everlasting penalty and an everlasting reward, but in both cases eternity is way out of proportion to a lifetime of, say, seventy years. Bestowing more recompense than has been earned may pass as generous, but inflicting more pain than has been deserved strikes as cruel.

I have listed five punishments. Are they separate ones for different offences, or are "left", "shut out" and "outer darkness" partial descriptions of one punishment - with "destroyed" applying to death, not the afterlife - and really anyone who does not go to heaven goes to hell? The latter fate appears the most likely. Jesus said that "all causes of sin and all evildoers" would be thrown into hell (Matt. 13, 41, 42, 49, 50); "Every tree that does not bear good fruit is cut down and thrown into the fire" (Matt. 7, 19. Com. Jn 15, 6); people who had not helped would so suffer (Matt. 25, 41), even anybody who calls his brother a fool "shall be liable to the hell of fire" (Matt. 5, 22).

Given such a demanding standard it is almost certain that everyone will do something which leads to hell; but it is just as certain that everyone will do something which leads to heaven. Our lives are a mixture of good and bad. I infer, therefore, that the judgement will be based on which of the two is, overall, predominant, with repentance offering another chance of salvation.

The prospect of eternal bliss or eternal torment depending on our beliefs and actions is, don't you think, worth our serious - and I stress, serious – consideration?

Theology: a summary

God is a particular entity, sentient and omnipotent. The only god, he is named the Lord. He resides in heaven which is above the earth. We should regard him as a father-figure who we can contact through prayer. Like a father, he provides for us and we should love and obey him.

Jesus is God's son. He pre-existed with his father. Jesus is the Christ, the Messiah. He came into the world to urge mankind to repent and be righteous. As predicted, he was killed, but rose. He will come again, separate good people from bad and establish God's kingdom universally.

The Holy Spirit enters a believer and provides inspiration, spontaneous speech and knowledge. It proceeds from the Father and is sent in the name of the Son. To speak against it is an unforgivable sin.

For salvation many conditions are stated. I summarise them as honour God and Jesus and practise their teachings. Whenever you fail, repent.

Who is to be saved and who condemned will be revealed on the day of judgement. The living will be, or have been, judged. Then is likely to be the time when the dead who were righteous are raised to life; whether the dead who were not righteous are raised is unclear.

Good people go to heaven where they live forever; bad people probably go to hell, a place of fire, where they suffer, probably forever.

Worship

Faith

Jesus spoke of faith as firm belief in his words, doubtless needed by "he who endures to the end" (Mk 13, 13); he prayed that Peter's would not fail (Lk 22, 31, 32), and even asked if he would find any when he returned to earth (Lk 18, 8). The gospels often relate faith to supernatural power. Some of the people Jesus miraculously cured, or those who acted on their behalf, he commended because they believed he could perform the miracle (Matt. 8, 10; 9, 22, 29; 15, 28; Mk 2, 5; Lk 17, 19). On the other hand, he criticised some because they did not believe enough. In the healing of the epileptic boy (Matt. 17, 14-20; Mk 9, 14-29; Lk 9, 37-43) he rebuked the father (Mk 9, 23), his disciples (Matt. 17, 20) and his generation (Lk 9, 41) for their lack of faith. The disciples were similarly reproached when they feared they might drown (Mk 4, 40.Com. Matt. 14, 31) and when they were concerned they might go hungry (Matt. 16, 8). To worry if God will provide shows "little faith" (Lk 12, 28).

"All things are possible to him who believes," (Mk 9, 23) Jesus stated, and "if you have faith and never doubt ... even if you say to this mountain, 'Be taken up and cast into the sea,' it will be done" (Matt. 21, 21); "If you had faith as a grain of mustard seed, you could say to this sycamine tree, 'Be rooted up, and be planted in the sea,' and it would obey you" (Lk 17, 6). I wonder if anyone has ever commanded either of these transposings and been successful. I suspect we are more likely to follow the course attributed to another prophet - "If the mountain won't come to Mohammed, Mohammed must go to the mountain". Yet before categorising Jesus' 'move into the sea' statements as hyperbole I note that the first one was spoken in the context of the fig tree withering when he forbade it to bear any more fruit (Matt. 21, 19). God was quite capable of moving mountains and trees. The Bible contains many miracles, over nature as well as over illness. There are the stories of the mountains being "rent" (1 Kings 19, 11) and of Aaron's rod being transformed into an almond tree (Numbers 17, 8). As someone who cured the sick, raised the dead, multiplied food, turned water into wine, walked on water and calmed a storm, Jesus may well have intended his illustrations of the possible to be taken literally. Incredible feats could be achieved, with faith.

Prayer

Jesus advocated praying, and it appears to have been important in his own life (e.g. Mk 1, 35; 6, 46; Lk 5, 16; 6, 12; 9, 28). John chapter 17 is one long prayer. In method, do not pray ostentatiously, "like the hypocrites" (Matt. 6, 5), but in private (Matt. 6, 6); do not be verbose, "Many words" (Matt. 6, 7) won't make more impact. The model is the Lord's prayer (Matt. 6, 9-13).

Prayers commonly include requests, really an unnecessary part since "your Father knows what you need before you ask him" (Matt. 6, 8). Indeed, all prayer is, strictly, unnecessary because God knows our thoughts. There is no need to put them into words. But perhaps the act is reassuring to the supplicant and pleasing to God, a welcome call! His own words about God's prescience did not dissuade Jesus from praying, and most of his recorded prayers contain entreaties. Experience shows that if something is asked for, it is not always given. "Ask, and it will be given you" (Matt. 7, 7) should be set against God will "give good things to those who ask him" (Matt. 7, 11) and, reasonably, he will decide which things are good. "Whatever you ask in my name, I will do it" (Jn 14, 13) should be tempered by, "If you abide in me, and my words abide in you, ask whatever you will, and it shall be done for you" (Jn 15, 7); not just Jesus' name, but also his wish, then your desire will be his desire. No doubt there are many cases where prayers seem to have been successful, and many cases where they have not; no response may leave even committed Christians profoundly perplexed and disappointed because their intent was so evidently beneficial. Then prayer must be supplemented by faith. God knows best.

Fasting

As with prayer, fasting was not to be practised ostenta-tiously, but as a secret between the abstainer and God (Matt. 6, 16-18). Though Jesus accepted the act, it fea-tures only once in his own life: he fasted forty days in preparation for his ministry (Matt. 4, 2). Thereafter he seems to concur with the observation that the disciples of John the Baptist and of the Pharisees fast, but his do not (Mk 2, 18), and it is likely he did not. There is his com-parison to a wedding and to himself as a bridegroom (Mk 2, 19). That is not the time to fast. When he is "taken away", then his disciples will fast (Mk 2, 20).

Whether he abstains or not, Jesus concludes that "the men of this generation" (Lk 7, 31) will find fault, "For John the Baptist has come eating no bread and drinking no wine; and you say, 'He has a demon'. The Son of man has come eating and drinking; and you say, 'Behold, a glutton and a drunkard …'" (Lk 7, 33, 34).

Sacrifices

Jesus told the leper he cured to "offer for your cleansing what Moses commanded" (Mk 1, 44; Leviticus 14, 10. Com. Lk 17, 14). Sacrifices were in the law and Jesus usually followed the law. They were in the ritual and he usually kept the ritual (Lk 4, 16; 22, 7, 8, 15; Jn 2, 13, 23; 5, 1; 7, 8 -10). More important than sacrifices, though, are virtues. If you are about to make an offering and remember that someone has a complaint against you, first resolve the problem, then submit your gift (Matt. 5, 23, 24). Twice Jesus draws on the prophet Hosea to declare, "I desire mercy, and not sacrifice" (Matt. 9, 13; 12, 7), which strictly implies that God doesn't want sacrifices at all, though Hosea proceeds to speak of a preference, not a prohibition ("… rather than … ", Hosea 6, 6); and, overall, by his conduct as well as by his words, Jesus indicates likewise, not proscribing but prioritising. When the scribe said that loving God and one's neighbour was "much more than … sacrifices … Jesus saw that he answered wisely" (Mk 12, 32-34). One of Jesus' many criticisms of the Pharisees was "… you tithe mint and dill and cummin, and have neglected the weightier matters of the law, justice and mercy and faith; these you ought to have done, without neglecting the others" (Matt. 23, 23). He might well have taught the same for sacrifices, perform them, but the performance of fairness, compassion and devotion matter more.

The Sabbath

The Sabbath day, the seventh, was one of rest remembering God resting on the seventh day of his creation of the universe (Exodus 20, 8-11. Genesis 2, 1 - 3). No work was to be done on that day (e.g. Exodus 31, 15). The gospels suggest that Jesus observed the Sabbath (e.g. Lk 4, 16), as he did the religious festivals (e.g. Jn 5, 1). In speaking of the calamities preceding his second coming he tells his disciples to "Pray that your flight may not be … on a Sabbath" (Matt. 24, 20), perhaps in deference to the stipulation that any journey on that day should be a short one - a Sabbath day's journey (Acts 1, 12, based on Joshua 3, 4) - or else it would amount to work.

The religious leaders, however, thought that Jesus did not observe the Sabbath sufficiently. They censured him for allowing his disciples to pluck grain (Matt. 12, 1 - 8) and for he himself performing miracles (Matt. 12, 9-14; Lk 13, 10-17; 14, 1-6; Jn 5, 2-17; 9, 1-16) on the day. The accusation appeared to be that he or his disciples were working (Lk 13, 14). Jesus didn't deny it. He answered with a variety of justifications: on the Sabbath there is essential work - owners water their animals (Lk 13, 15); there may be emergencies - owners may have to rescue their animals (Lk 14, 5) and, another, when he was hungry David broke the law (Matt. 12, 3, 4); there are rituals - "the priests in the temple profane the Sabbath, and are guiltless" (Matt. 12, 5), they circumcise then, why be angry if Jesus makes "a man's whole body well" (Jn 7, 23) then? "Is it lawful on the Sabbath to do good or to do harm … ?" (Mk 3, 4) - another justification, on the day of rest spontaneous acts of helpfulness are permissible.

These may be sensible exceptions, and one (Lk, 14, 6), if not all, silenced Jesus' critics (Lk 13, 17). But, infuriated (Lk 6, 11), they plotted to destroy him (Mk 3, 6). So he was courting danger when he also spoke of status as vindicating actions - "the Son of man is lord even of the Sabbath" (Mk 2, 28), therefore he could decide what could be done on the day; his hearers may not have understood the Son of man to mean himself, but, whoever it was, for them there was only one lord of the Sabbath, the Lord. Another perilous statement was, "The Sabbath was made for man, not man for the Sabbath" (Mk 2, 27) which could be interpreted as men in general can order the day. Bearing in mind Jesus' regard for God's law and his own respect for the Sabbath, he probably meant no more than, that day was made for the benefit of man. But emphasising men could loosen their obligations to the day. Being "persecuted" (Jn 5, 16) for curing a man on the Sabbath (Jn 5, 2-9), Jesus fanned the flames by declaring, on the day of rest itself, "My Father is working still, and I am working" (Jn 5, 17). "This was why the Jews sought all the more to kill him, because he not only broke the Sabbath but also called God his Father, making himself equal with God" (Jn 5, 18. Com. Jn 10, 30-33; 19, 7).

To my mind most of Jesus' answers to working on the Sabbath were convincing, but his references to his own authority and his hint of men's, were incendiary to his adversaries, and stand in contrast to the idea that for at least the first part of his ministry he tried to play down his identity, to avoid trouble - "the messianic secret".

Worship: a summary

As described in the gospels, faith is not just belief, but also the strength of the belief. Is it strong enough to accept the teaching wholeheartedly, to withstand persecution and to be convinced that God will grant any miracle if he wishes?

Prayer is commended, and prayers often contain personal requests. Ask with Jesus' approval and it will be given.

As with praying, fasting is to be undertaken without show. Jesus indicated his disciples would fast later, not whilst he was with them.

Offer sacrifices, but first come feelings, principles and general conduct.

Jesus observed the Sabbath as a time of worship, but he pointed out work that is done, and would be if need be, on that day. He suggested immediate acts of helpfulness are permitted. His own unique status allowed him to override the Sabbath law.

Morality

The Fundamental Commandments

The first commandment is "'… you shall love the Lord your God with all your heart, and with all your soul, and with all your mind, and with all your strength'. The second is this, 'You shall love your neighbour as yourself'. There is no other commandment greater than these" (Mk 12, 30, 31). Love! Jesus begins and builds on a feeling. Love God and your neighbour, then act accordingly. If you love God you will naturally want to express it, in prayer and worship, in what you say about him to others and in what you do which should be his will. If you love your neighbour you are concerned about their welfare and you will help them should the need arise. A parable - perhaps the most famous in the gospels - which illustrates neighbourliness is The Good Samaritan (Lk 10, 29-37) and it points to your neighbour as being anyone. The victim is described simply as "a man "(Lk 10, 30); the Samaritan does not ask what sort of man. To "love your neighbour as yourself" (Mk 12, 31) is complemented by another commandment, "whatever you wish that men would do to you, do so to them … "(Matt. 7, 12). So brief and yet so comprehensive! The very core and also the very limit of social morality!

With such pronouncements it is not surprising that the word 'love' has been taken to epitomise Christianity (see 1 John 4, 8). But Christians do not love everything. They hate sin and there are many acts which are sinful. So long as a person wilfully transgresses he is censured (Lk 12, 47). In the face of sin, love is manifested not by excusing and ignoring, but by criticising, persuading, cajoling, imploring, striving to bring about change; if a sinner does not reform, and is more bad than good, then when he comes to God's judgement he will be condemned and punished, probably forever. He is "cursed" (Matt. 25, 41). That too is a fundamental part of Christianity. Love has its limits.

The Law

"Did not Moses give you the law?" Jesus asked the Jews (Jn 7, 19), the law of Moses dictated to him by God (e.g. Exodus 24, 12). Jesus had not come to "abolish" it, but to "fulfil" it (Matt. 5, 17) and to the letter, "not an iota, not a dot, will pass from the law until all is accomplished" (Matt. 5, 18). Anyone who "relaxes one of the least of these commandments and teaches men so, shall be called least in the kingdom of heaven ..." (Matt. 5, 19). Given such resounding endorsement, it is strange that within the same speech, 'the sermon on the mount,' Jesus changed one apparent law and one actual law into their very opposites: "'... hate your enemy'" (Matt. 5, 43. Com. Exodus 23, 22; Deuteronomy 32, 41; 33, 27) becomes "Love your enemies" (Matt. 5, 44) and "'An eye for an eye ...'" (Matt. 5, 38. Deuteronomy 19, 21) becomes turn the other cheek (Matt. 5, 39). Assuming a man should not make his wife "an adulteress" (Matt. 5, 32), Jesus almost changed divorce from permitted (Deuteronomy 24, 1-4) to prohibited except, he qualified, for "unchastity" (Matt. 5, 32); and though retaining the laws themselves he greatly extended three more: not only don't kill (Exodus 20, 13) but even don't be angry (Matt. 5, 21, 22), not only don't commit adultery (Exodus 20, 14) but also don't be lustful (Matt. 5, 27, 28) and not only don't swear falsely (Leviticus 19, 12; Numbers 30, 2) but don't swear at all (Matt. 5, 33-37).

In declaring you should love your enemy; if struck, invite another strike; don't be angry with anyone and never cast a lustful look, Jesus raises moral expectations to an impossible level, or virtually so. Innate feelings and responses must be crushed. They become a sin. No wonder the church holds that we are all sinners, and considering these injunctions in relation to Jesus himself, I wonder what love he had for blasphemers (Mk 3, 29), for those who lead a child astray (Mk 9, 42) and for Judas Iscariot (Mk 14, 21). When he himself was struck he asked why (Jn 18, 22, 23) and where his parables end with violent punishment (e.g. The Wicked Tenants, Mk 12, 1-9) he speaks as though that is fitting (e.g. Mk 12, 9). He certainly seemed to be angry when he drove the traders out of the temple (Jn 2, 14-16) and when he denounced the scribes and Pharisees (Matt. 23), calling them worse than fools (Matt. 5, 22; 23, 33). During his castigation of the religious leaders Jesus noted the correct things to swear by (Matt. 23, 16-22); he did not ban oaths altogether (Matt. 5, 34). Is one of his own favourite phrases, "Truly, I say to you ..." (e.g. Mk 11, 23), an oath, or at least an unnecessary elaboration (Matt. 5, 37)? Measured by his new rules it appears that on occasions Jesus 'slipped' or there is the rather bewildering possibility that there are two codes of conduct, one for God and Jesus, the other for mankind, or that these great demands are really great overstatements.

I have focused on 'the sermon on the mount'. As he stated so definitely in that sermon Jesus espoused the Mosaic law. In the temptations (Matt. 4, 1-11) he answered the devil from the book of Deuteronomy (8, 3; 6, 16; 6, 13). He instructed the leper to "offer the gift that Moses commanded" (Matt. 8, 4. Com. Lk 17, 14).

Sensitive to accusations that he was altering or breaking the law, he suggested that Moses disagreed with divorce really (Mk 10, 5). Jesus justified his working on the Sabbath. He told the Pharisees they were transgressing the command to honour parents (Matt. 15, 3, 4). They were neglecting "the weightier matters of the law" (Matt. 23, 23). All in all, they had left "the commandment of God" (Mk 7, 8. Com. Jn 7, 19). Since the Pharisees "sit on Moses' seat" (Matt. 23, 2) the people were to do what they said, but not what they did (Matt. 23, 3). Love God and your neighbour are both instructions from the law (Deuteronomy 6, 5; Leviticus 19, 18). When he was asked what must be done "to inherit eternal life" (Mk 10, 17), Jesus reminded the man of "the commandments" (Mk 10, 19) and recited six of them, five from the Decalogue (Mk 10, 19). During 'the last supper' he told his disciples that he had "kept my Father's commandments" (Jn 15, 10). These many references to the law and to obeying it, spread throughout the gospels, make his radical transforming of some laws, during 'the sermon on the mount', an oddity, which could be explained as a zealous outburst, maybe prompted by the opportunity and atmosphere of the occasion, addressing "a great multitude" (Lk 6, 17). Accepting this exegesis myself, I am suggesting that Jesus ' got carried away'. He overdid it. The demands to quell God-given nature, respond to every adversity with love and forgiveness and pointedly invite further affliction come across as unreasonable in themselves and contrary to other teachings and actions in the gospels.

Associated with the law were traditions, man-made additions. Verses 3 and 4 of Mark chapter 7 list some concerning hygiene. When asked why his disciples did not wash their hands before eating (Mk 7, 5), Jesus told his disapprovers, "You leave the commandment of God, and hold fast the tradition of men" (Mk 7, 8). "Many" of the traditions made "void the word of God" (Mk 7, 13), and he cited as an example the "rejecting" (Mk 7, 9) of the commandment to honour parents by a son telling his parents that what they would have gained from him is instead given to God, thus "you no longer permit him to do anything for his father or mother" (Mk 7, 12). The thought arises, what did Jesus do for his parents? There are a couple of recorded incidents, turning water into wine (Jn 2, 1-11) and suggesting, belatedly, some arrangement for Mary's future (Jn 19, 26, 27). However, with his family wanting to speak to him, he said his mother and brothers were those who sat around him, they were, "Whoever does the will of God" (Mk 3, 31-35). Similarly, when an onlooker blessed his mother Jesus responded with, "Blessed rather are those who hear the word of God and keep it!" (Lk 11, 27, 28). His parents seem to mean no more to him than anyone else. His family was those who served God. A person who "does not hate his own father and mother … cannot be my disciple" (Lk 14, 26). Hyperbole, I take it, but still scarcely a call to help them. Didn't Jesus give what his parents would have gained from him to God?

Good thoughts and deeds

Love is the starting - point. "You shall love your neighbour as yourself" (Mk 12, 31); "whatever you wish that men would do to you, do so to them" (Matt. 7, 12); love, even, "your enemies" (Matt. 5, 44). I question, though, if love is really the most accurate word to denote how one person should regard another because it is suggestive of the very height of affection, a deep desire and a manifest pleasure to be with and to cherish. So often it is used to describe a relationship between certain individuals, especially, of course, lovers. One may say Jesus' whole motivation was love, but not the sort I have just characterised - the most explicit portrayal of that kind was with the sisters Mary and Martha and their brother Lazarus (Jn 11, 3,5,11, 28, 33, 35, 36, 38). There may have been a similar bond between Jesus and his disciples (e.g. Jn 13, 34); the gospels say little about their informal life. Towards people in general though I would say love would be more precisely defined as concern or compassion. Jesus was concerned that men and women should be saved. He was mindful of the poor and needy (e.g. Matt. 25, 35, 36; Mk 10, 21; Lk 4, 17-21; Jn 13, 29). In particular, he helped by performing, apparently, a great many miracles (e.g. Mk 6, 54-56). He had compassion on the 5,000 who he fed (Matt. 14, 14) and on the widow of Nain whose only son had just died (Lk 7, 13). Whichever word is chosen, however, I emphasise that it does not encapsulate the whole story. There were times when Jesus was vitriolic. In the very verses advocating love he is disparaging about "tax collectors" (Matt. 5, 46) and "Gentiles" (Matt. 5, 47). He compared the Syrophoenician woman to a dog (Mk 7, 27) and called Peter "Satan" (Mk 8, 33). The religious leaders and lawyers were lambasted at length and in the most scathing terminology (e.g. Lk 11, 39-52). There are those who no matter what their future conduct are already doomed -people who have blasphemed against the Holy Spirit (Mk 3, 29), people who have caused a child who believes in Jesus to sin (Mk 9, 42) and, at the time, Judas

Iscariot (Mk 14, 21); and there will be others who are eventually condemned to hell, most likely for eternity.

The Old Testament law stipulated nurturing good relations with "your neighbour" (Leviticus 19,17, 18); helping him if he fell on hard times (Leviticus 25, 35-41); helping, in some ways at least, your enemy (Exodus 23, 4, 5). It prescribed, especially, caring for the poor, sojourners, fatherless and widows (e.g. Exodus 23, 10, 11; Leviticus 19, 9, 10; Deuteronomy 10, 18), and the prophets took up these themes (e.g. Isaiah 10, 1, 2; Jeremiah 7, 5-7; Ezekiel 22, 6, 7; Amos 2, 6, 7; Zechariah 7, 8-10; Malachi 3, 5). Philanthropy was expected, and so Jesus nearly always taught. He condemned "the goats" because they did not give food or drink, they did not welcome or clothe or visit (Matt. 25, 31-46. Com. Ezekiel 34, 4). They might have kept every law forbidding this and that, but they did not assist the needy. In the parable of The Sower the good "are the ones who hear the word and accept it and bear fruit, thirtyfold and sixtyfold and a hundredfold" (Mk 4, 20). "Bear fruit"! I think the only reasonable interpretation of this metaphor is, put the gospel into practice and that includes do good deeds (com. Jn 15, 8-10; Matt. 7, 15-20). Making more of what you are given is clearly the point of the parables of The Talents (Matt. 25, 14-30) and of The Pounds (Lk 19, 12-27). Again, be fruitful! Assuming Jesus did not really intend, make as much money as possible - the very opposite of his direction on the subject - then I take the money given to represent the teaching and the extra returned not to represent more teaching, which would be unauthorised, but the extent to which one has fulfilled the original expectations. Everyone is required to show results. The servant who didn't make more was to be "cast ... into the outer darkness" (Matt. 25, 30). Yet he protected what he had been given and handed it back whole. He did nothing wrong with it. This may stand for a person not being bad, but not purposefully doing good; for negative observance, but not positive action. So, not only don't harm; also, help!

One particular good deed is, convert other people. Jesus told Simon and Andrew that they would "become fishers of men" (Mk 1, 16, 17) and at his ascension he commanded his disciples to "Go ... and make disciples" (Matt. 28, 19). Out of duty and out of desire, the new believers, in turn, try to make more believers. Converting others and being rewarded may lie in the imagery in John chapter 4 verses 35-38 - harvest, reap, wages, fruit, eternal life. When Jesus sent the seventy into the towns around "harvest" surely stands for people and the "labourers" most likely for missionaries (Lk 10, 1-12). The gospel should be spread, for everyone's sake.

Bad thoughts and deeds

"What comes out of a man is what defiles a man" (Mk 7, 20) and this includes "evil thoughts" (Mk 7, 21) such as of lust (Matt. 5, 28), coveting, envy and pride (Mk 7, 22); also, either as thoughts or actions are "wickedness" and "foolishness" (Mk 7, 22). Whether bad thoughts are as grave as bad deeds is not stated, nor at what point a normal thought becomes a bad one: sexual interest, wishing we had what somebody else has and being proud of something are intrinsic parts of human nature. Perhaps Jesus meant they become bad when they become deep-rooted - not just sexual attraction, but longing and fantasising; not just a passing fancy to have the same, but a strong desire fostering resentment and maliciousness, and not just pride in a particular instance, but general self-adulation and ostentation (com. Matt. 23, 5-7; Lk 18, 9-14). Jesus may have had in mind such excesses, but he does not draw the boundaries.

Of course, evil thoughts can become evil deeds. Jesus listed false witness (Matt. 15, 19), fornication, theft, murder, adultery, deceit, licentiousness and slander (Mk 7, 21, 22). He told the rich man, "'Do not kill, Do not commit adultery, Do not steal, Do not bear false witness, Do not defraud, Honour your father and mother'" (Mk 10, 19). In short, keep "the commandments" (Mk 10,19), the law of Moses, which also included thoughts amongst the deeds - within the Ten Commandments are, honour parents (Exodus 20, 12) and don't covet (Exodus 20, 17). As noted, Jesus himself changed a few laws; presumably, though, without his expressed, specific approval, not to obey the Mosaic code is bad.

Forgiving

In his longest teaching about people forgiving each other (Matt. 18, 15-17) Jesus makes forgiveness dependent on the wrongdoer recognising his fault. Just afterwards, however, he tells Peter he should forgive repeatedly and there is no mention of acknowledging fault (Matt. 18, 21, 22). Again, the Lord's prayer speaks of "forgive" (Matt. 6, 12; Lk 11, 4), but not of guilt, and Jesus stated, without qualification, that if you forgive others, God will forgive you (Matt. 6, 14; Mk 11, 25; Lk 6, 37c) - a statement I query since, as argued, many qualities are needed for salvation. One teaching, then, requires confession before forgiveness, and another, which does not mention any response by the offender, presents the possibility that we should forgive regardless. But God does not forgive regardless. He demands repentance. It follows then that if God requires one person to forgive another without the offender even accepting blame let alone showing remorse, God requires a moral standard not practised by he himself, and a standard that is unnatural since if we are wronged we expect redress, and unjust since if we are wronged we deserve redress; the injustice should be righted.

In 'the sermon on the mount' which allows for open-ended forgiveness (e.g. Matt. 6, 14) and includes "turn" the other cheek (Matt. 5, 39), Jesus also presents a situation where one person "has something against" (Matt. 5, 23) another, and he does not say that the accuser should forgive, but that the accused should seek reconciliation lest he "be put in prison; truly, I say to you, you will never get out till you have paid the last penny" (Matt. 5, 25, 26). No forgiveness there! The conclusions of the parables of The Wicked Tenants (Mk 12, 9), The Unmerciful Servant (Matt. 18, 34), The Marriage Feast (Matt. 22, 7), The Faithful and Unfaithful Steward (Lk 12, 46) and The Pounds (Lk 19, 24) are not of forgiveness, but punishment. Of course, parables are stories and one cannot say that Jesus agreed with the outcome of the stories; these may well represent God's judgement, not man's, though God, through Moses, demanded that men too should administer justice and impose penalties, including death. The punishments cited in these parables are commensurate with the crimes, and Jesus seems to deliver them with passion. It may be that he did agree with them. The last verse of the parable of The Unmerciful

Servant is, "So also my heavenly Father will do to every one of you …" (Matt. 18, 35). Given that God may not do exactly what the king did, he appears to approve of what the king did.

Luke's gospel has a version of Matthew 18, 15-17, 21, 22, and to be forgiven, one or many times, repentance is required (Lk 17, 3, 4). These detailed words, in Matthew and Luke, have priority over far fewer ones which do not say if they mean forgive regardless of remorse. The prospect of unconditional forgiveness may have arisen quite simply because Jesus did not say enough. He didn't add the necessary qualification of repentance, and if he had done so still that would not suffice between men and men for if society routinely pardoned its transgressors because they expressed sorrow wouldn't many take advantage?

Enemies

"Love your enemies and pray for those who persecute you" (Matt. 5, 44), perhaps in the manner of Jesus at his crucifixion, "Father, forgive them; for they know not what they do" (Lk 23, 34). Whether they act from ignorance or malice, love them, but, I say again, not their sin and if they persist in sin they themselves will eventually be punished, horrifically. "Love your enemies … so that you may be sons of your Father … for he makes his sun rise on the evil and on the good …" (Matt. 5, 44, 45). I take it, however, that when judgement comes the sun will no longer rise on the evil for "your Father" will condemn and consign them to hell, those who are unrepentant sinners and those who have committed an unforgivable sin. They have performed the work of God's arch-enemy, Satan, and the only love they, and Satan, may receive is that of sadness and regret. Whilst there is a chance of redemption love your enemy by doing all you can to transform and save him - this really demonstrates your care, your love.

Non-resistance

"Do not resist one who is evil" (Matt. 5, 39). Indeed, facilitate more evil; so, "... if anyone strikes you on the right cheek, turn to him the other also; and if anyone would sue you and take your coat, let him have your cloak as well; and if anyone forces you to go one mile, go with him two miles" (Matt. 5, 39-41. Com. Lk 6, 29). Perhaps these are signs that you love your enemy (Lk 6, 27) and you are trying to persuade him - now hopefully disconcerted by your response - to change his ways. You want him to realise that what he is doing is wrong; otherwise you are condoning and compounding the wrong. You want him to repent.

When Jesus himself was struck (Jn 18, 22) we are not told whether he turned the other cheek, but perhaps he didn't since we are told that he protested (Jn 18, 23). Verbally, he was always full of fight. He stoutly answered his critics (e.g. Mk 2, 23-27) and he vehemently chastised the religious leaders (e.g. Matt. 23, 27), the Jews (e.g. Jn 7, 19), Jerusalem (e.g. Matt. 23, 37), Chorazin, Bethsaida and Capernaum (Lk 10, 13-15), his generation (e.g. Lk 11, 29) and the world (e.g. Jn 7, 7). Though blessing the peacemakers (Matt. 5, 9), he "came to cast fire upon the earth" (Lk 12, 49), to give "division" rather than "peace" (Lk 12, 51) for his teaching would divide households, one member against another (Lk 12, 52, 53). Opposed, indeed persecuted, his followers, like himself, were to stand firm (Mk 13, 13). He generally rejected force, but he did set about the sellers in the temple (Jn 2, 14, 15). To these extents Jesus engaged in conflict. He resisted evil and it is fundamental to his teaching that everybody else should too. There is the story of him confronting Satan, the supreme evil one, head - on (Matt. 4, 1-11).

To turn the other cheek permits injustice and runs the risk of exploitation. If practised, people could assault each other and they would be invited to assault more. They commit a wrong and they might not repent. There would be ongoing personal and social harm. Societies, including those professing to be Christian, follow, rather, the maxim of "An eye for an eye ..." (Matt. 5, 38), and though God may endure many sins he also exacts punishment eventually. Turning the other cheek could be an impressive expression of love, but for humans and for God love is not limitless.

Giving

Following his call not to resist, Jesus moves on to, "Give to him who begs from you, and do not refuse him who would borrow from you" (Matt. 5, 42); moreover, "lend, expecting nothing in return" (Lk 6, 35), which is tantamount to giving unless the recipient wishes to repay you. So, give and lend whenever you are asked. Elsewhere, though, Jesus also says, "... you always have the poor with you, and whenever you will, you can do good to them" (Mk 14, 7). So giving is a matter of choice, as you wish. The latter quotation was part of Jesus' answer to the objection that expensive nard had just been squandered, by being poured over his head

(Mk 14, 3-5), and he does refer to himself in particular, but these words are general and embody a new teaching, albeit a possible over-reaction in his defence of the act. Whatever the case, they stand on their own. In the main Jesus taught that people should give: "sell what you have, and give to the poor" (Mk 10, 21); "Sell your possessions, and give alms" (Lk 12, 33) and "… when you give a feast, invite the poor, the maimed, the lame, the blind" (Lk 14, 13).

There is a suggestion that the more you give now the more you will receive in heaven (Lk 6, 38) but the story of the widow's offering (Mk 12, 41-44) shows that this is to be understood not purely quantitatively, but as the amount bestowed in proportion to the amount possessed. Giving of your substance indicates more concern than giving of your excess - you are parting with what really matters to you. The widow's "two copper coins" (Mk 12, 42) were far more prized than the rich people's "large sums" (Mk 12, 41).

If people really did give on request, considering how many requests they receive, through the various channels, it might necessitate giving very little to each or risk falling into poverty themselves. They could become beggars. Hopefully, someone would give to them, then they could give to others and there would form a circle of have, give, beg, have, give, beg, ad infinitum. Accepting that Christians are expected to give, to what extent, realistically?

Wealth

"Do not lay up for yourselves treasures on earth … but lay up for yourselves treasure in heaven" (Matt. 6,

19, 20) - don't accumulate earthly, but spiritual wealth, perform God's will and your deeds will be rewarded in heaven. Material possessions are not the yardstick (Lk 12, 15); they are damaged and stolen (Matt. 6, 19); they are transitory, left at death, and that may be sooner than anticipated (Lk 12, 16-20). A place in heaven, on the other hand, lasts forever. "You cannot serve God and mammon" (wealth) (Lk 16, 13); that is like a man trying to serve two masters - "he will hate the one and love the other" (Lk 16, 13). These alternatives are extreme. Surely it doesn't have to be a matter of love or hate, but it is a matter of what is most important, "where your treasure is, there will your heart be also" (Matt. 6, 21). God or riches? If your priority is riches you will prove "unfruitful" (Mk 4, 19) for God. Then, presumably, you will be condemned and "what does it profit a man to gain the whole world and forfeit his life?" (Mk 8, 36). Therefore, "Do not labour for the food which perishes, but for the food which endures to eternal life" (Jn 6, 27). Do not try to be wealthy; strive to be righteous.

Jesus told the rich man to "go, sell what you have, and give to the poor ..." (Mk 10, 21), which the man would not bring himself to do. Some of the ideas implied in this story are actually at variance with each other. Jesus may have meant the man should renounce his riches if he "would be perfect", as Matthew expresses it (Matt. 19, 21), though by keeping the commandments he has done enough to inherit eternal life. If this is the meaning - which does not take account of belief in Jesus - then the righteous rich can enter heaven. Jesus proceeds to say it will be "hard" (Mk 10, 23) - he doesn't say impossible - for the rich to go into the kingdom of God; but then he as good as says, by his famous camel through the eye of a needle comparison (Mk 10, 25), that entry will be impossible, given a normal camel and a normal needle. The disciples are astonished, exclaiming, "Then who can be saved?" (Mk 10, 26) - a reaction I find in itself rather astonishing since I would expect them to know what is crucial, especially if this event occurred towards the end of the ministry. Jesus answers that "... all things are possible with God" (Mk 10, 27) which seems to accept their response and, in this context, raises the prospect that somehow God can rightly bring the wealthy into heaven. All somewhat perplexing! Amongst the twists and turns, though, the most definite statements (Mk 10, 17, 21, 25) imply that riches prohibit eternal life.

It may be supposed that when Jesus bid the rich man to sell his belongings he intended only him, but the instruction was also issued generally - "Sell your possessions, and give alms" (Lk 12, 33), spoken to "his disciples" (Lk 12, 22) and perhaps to "the multitude" (Lk 12, 1); "whoever of you does not renounce all that he has cannot be my disciple" (Lk 14, 33), spoken to "great multitudes" (Lk 14, 25), and raising the same problem as with "Giving" - how, then, do you live? Jesus preached "good news to the poor" (Lk 4, 18, 21; 7, 22), they are "Blessed" (Lk 6, 20), theirs "is the kingdom of God" (Lk 6, 20). "But woe to you that are rich, for you have received your consolation" (Lk 6, 24), a pronouncement vividly enacted in the story of the rich man and Lazarus (Lk 16, 19-31) - "Son, remember that you in your lifetime received your good things, and Lazarus in like manner evil things; but now he is comforted here, and you are in anguish" (Lk 16, 25).

It is inevitable, therefore, that if you are wealthy in this life you will suffer in the next. This teaching is crystal clear. "Woe to you that are full now, for you shall hunger" (Lk 6, 25). If you are already wealthy, give your riches to the poor.

What, then, is to be understood by, "... to him who has will more be given; and from him who has not, even what he has will be taken away" (Mk 4, 25)? Given the preceding evidence, these words do not apply to material possessions. They come shortly after the meaning of the parable of The Sower which urges fruitfulness, "thirtyfold and sixtyfold and a hundred fold" (Mk 4, 20), and expressly mentions riches as preventing it (Mk 4, 19). The kind of fruitfulness Jesus meant stands out as practising "the word" (Mk 4, 20), that is, his teaching - and within it he plainly taught, don't be wealthy. 'Have and be given' and 'Give and be given' can both be generalised as, do good and you will be rewarded. With all this in mind, I find the themes of the parables of The Talents (Matt. 25, 14 -30) and of The Pounds (Lk 19, 12-27) - multiply money - distinctly out of place. I can only conclude that they too really refer to good works - like The Sower, be fruitful, fulfil "the word" (Mk 4, 20). Their context is, waiting for the kingdom of God (Matt. 25, 1, 5, 14; Lk 19, 11, 12); whilst waiting do not make yourself as rich as possible, but obey Jesus' instructions -religious and moral - as much as possible. When he returns everyone is expected to show results, good deeds not goods. Any notion that Jesus promoted affluence is simply overwhelmed by his teaching - and his own personal lifestyle - to the contrary. Reject wealth, totally; it is fatal, no less.

Judging

In 'the sermon on the mount' Jesus directed not judging at all, "Judge not, that you be not judged" (Matt. 7, 1). Considering that we make many judgements each day, about all kinds of things, perhaps he was thinking of what he proceeded to concentrate on, judging others and pinpointing their faults before recognising our own much bigger ones - start with ours, "first take the log out of your own eye, and then you will see clearly to take the speck out of your brother's eye" (Matt. 7, 5). Therefore, judge! Of course, our shortcomings really may be fewer than theirs, and we can justly say they have "the log" and we "the speck" or the difference may be narrow and debatable or we might indeed not scrutinise ourselves sufficiently and if we did, realise that we are more at fault. There are many possible variations.

Not judging at all and so not being judged cannot on its own guarantee entry to heaven since, I note again, there is more than one requirement and given all of them, still the bad committed might outweigh the good. God and Jesus themselves must judge to assess who is and isn't to be admitted, so in telling people to refrain from judging Jesus is once more expecting them to follow a principle which God and he do not. In reality it is only sensible that people judge each other to some extent in their daily dealings and much more so in the forming of their relationships. Christians are duty-bound to be wary of evil influences. They should be able to recognise and rebuke what is bad. Be mindful of "False Christs and false prophets" (Mk 13, 22). They must judge others.

Again in 'the sermon on the mount' Jesus cautioned that the standards you apply when judging will be applied to you (Matt. 7, 2). It follows then that if you have been tolerant, God will be tolerant with you; if rigorous, likewise. Perversely, this leads to a person who strives to be a good Christian, setting high standards for himself and others, finding it more difficult to pass God's judgement than a person who is not so scrupulous. Surely, of the two, it should be the other way round. Fairest of all, people should be judged on one scale, God's, not on each of theirs.

Jesus judges (Jn 5, 22, 27, 30) and the disciples will too (Jn 20, 23; Lk 22, 30). He rebuked the religious leaders for neglecting justice (Matt. 23, 23) and told the crowds to judge for themselves (Lk 12, 57) and to do so "with right judgement" (Jn 7, 27). Nearly always Jesus did prescribe judging and really it cannot be avoided. First though, judge yourself, acknowledge your own imperfections and then you will "see … your brother's" (Matt. 7, 3) in proportion. It is a sobering point and a characteristic of - and a cue for - humility.

Humility

Live without display. "Beware of practising your piety before men in order to be seen by them" (Matt. 6, 1). Showiness will nullify piety (Matt. 6, 1). So, give alms "in secret" (Matt. 6, 4), pray in private (Matt. 6, 6) and in fasting show no sign of it (Matt. 6, 17, 18). Jesus condemned the scribes for their ostentation and self-importance (Mk 12, 38-40). In the parable of The Pharisee and the Tax Collector (Lk 18, 9-14) he contrasted the Pharisee's satisfaction and sense of superiority with the tax collector's plea for mercy; the latter was nearer the mark. "... everyone who exalts himself will be humbled, but he who humbles himself will be exalted" (Lk 18, 14).

"If anyone would be first, he must be last of all and servant of all" (Mk 9, 35) and "whoever would be great among you must be your servant, and whoever would be first among you must be slave of all" (Mk 10, 43, 44). Both of these quotations were responses to disciples seeking greatness, the highest positions of all, and Jesus used the same extreme terms. He did not initiate the idea. He was not advocating make yourself great. But his words could propel someone into making themselves as servile as possible so as to become as renowned as possible; and at one point Jesus himself taught such behaviour - in the parable of The Marriage Feast (Lk 14, 7-11) he says, "... when you are invited, go and sit in the lowest place, so that when your host comes he may say to you, 'Friend, go up higher'; then you will be honoured in the presence of all who sit at table with you" (Lk 14, 10)! Deliberately be low "so that" (Lk 14, 10) you will become high. Beware though lest then you are humbled because your intention was to be exalted. The subject turns circular.

Now self-interest is intrinsic. Every believer wants to go to heaven and strives accordingly. But he must be careful of preoccupation with self; that could distort his motivation, inducing him to act more for the sake of advantage than for the sake of righteousness. Extreme servility is as noticeable as extreme pomp so in its own way it draws the charge of self-display. Competing to be better than others runs the risk of lack of "love" (Mk 12, 31), pride, jealousy and malice (Mk 7, 21-23). The gospels do not usually portray humility as a race to the bottom. Simply, be humble, perhaps, like the tax collector (Lk 18, 13), in recognition of one's own failings. Do not seek the applause of men, but the approval of God and he "will reward you" (Matt. 6, 4, 6).

It may be observed that Jesus drew attention to himself. Was that ostentation ? No, because he needed to be heard so he had to be noticed. There was no alternative. Wanting people to believe that he was the Messiah and the Son of God, no less, offering eternal life, he had to reveal these stupendous claims too, and in substantiating them the miracles were very persuasive (e.g. Jn 11, 45-48). It was taken for granted that the Messiah would fulfil what was written in the Old Testament. This may explain why Jesus rode into Jerusalem on a colt (Matt. 21, 1-11, especially verses 4 and 5), a fulfilment of Zechariah chapter 9 verse 9. Given his reputation, the scriptural connection, and the religious occasion, the celebration of the Passover, Jesus' rapturous reception was a natural, impromptu salutation, though his refusal to restrain it (Lk 19, 39, 40) could be seen as self- indulgent. Jesus taught do not parade yourself and with one or two questionable exceptions (Jn 1, 48 ?) he practised what he preached on the matter.

Commitment

Total commitment - leading to eternal life - is most important. "The whole world" cannot compensate for it (Mk 8, 36, 37). Differences of belief may divide families (Matt. 10, 35, 36) and impel believers to leave their homes (Mk 10, 29). They should love Jesus more than their relatives (Matt. 10, 37). Understood! Though when Jesus said that they should "hate" their relatives (Lk 14, 26) I presume he was speaking not literally but provocatively, delivering a striking statement needing to be unravelled. Hate, also, one's "own life" (Lk 14, 26); Jesus says much the same in John's gospel where he adds "in this world" (Jn 12, 25). "Woe to the world for temptations to sin!" (Matt. 18, 7). Sin - that stands out as the nub of the matter; really, that is what believers should hate, not God-given lives, not people they have been told to love and try to save. But families might embody distractions, waywardness, even comfort and complacency, all of which stunt the work of God. Pinpointing relatives and speaking of them as the foe highlights the choice that a believer might have to make, natural family or God's family and for his inner self, the joys of the world or of heaven.

Jesus made this choice and, I have suggested, he treated his natural family not with hatred but with detachment. Basically, they were as others - his mother and siblings were those who did God's will (Mk 3, 35); not blessed be his mother but rather those who keep God's word (Lk 11, 27, 28); his words from the cross to his mother, though concerning her welfare, were extremely brief, factual and cold (Jn 19, 26). "And call no man your father on earth, for you have one Father, who is in heaven" (Matt. 23, 9), a dictum he may have applied even as a child (Lk 2, 49). His family was overridden by God and his mission. Such was his commitment. His answers to the willing follower who asked to first bury his father and to another who asked to first say farewell to those at home (Lk 9, 59-62) come across as heartless. Clearly, for the recruit who sets out there is to be no looking back (Lk 9, 62).

And the road ahead is as hard as it can be. It involves a man denying himself and taking up his cross (Mk 8, 34). Family discord, because of a member's different beliefs, may run so deeply that one relative "will deliver up" another "and have them put to death" (Matt. 10, 21). Indeed, adherents "will be hated by all for my name's sake" (Matt. 10, 22). They will be flogged (Matt. 10, 17) and "dragged" before rulers where they will "bear testimony" (Matt. 10, 18). Their killers will think they are serving God (Jn 16, 2). But blessed are those who are persecuted "on my account" (Matt. 5, 11). Their "reward is great in heaven" (Matt. 5, 12). "... he who endures to the end will be saved" (Matt. 24, 13).

What of Christians who don't endure to the end? Jesus refers to those who "immediately ... fall away" when "persecution arises" (Mk 4, 17); "... they have no root in themselves" (Mk 4, 17). But doubtless there are many who have tried to withstand, but eventually succumbed to pressure; because of it, they have renounced their faith verbally, though not in their heart. Surely God understands and admits them to heaven, providing they are acceptable overall. Nor do the gospels consider Christians who, on the other hand, far from suffering oppression enjoy preferment as members of an established church and live and die in peace and plenitude. It seems that Jesus did not envisage official approval. He expected his return to be within the lifetime of "this generation" (Mk 13, 30) and he anticipated opposition continuing to the day itself - wars, persecution, defilement, cosmic disturbances and then the coming of the Son of man (Matt. 24; Mk 13; Lk 21).

Divorce

Asked whether divorce was lawful Jesus drew on the book of Genesis (especially 1, 27; 2, 24) to imply that marriage was a relationship ordained by God, and divorce was not allowed (Matt. 19, 3 - 6). "What therefore God has joined together, let no man put asunder" (Matt. 19, 6). Nonetheless he made one exception, for "unchastity" (Matt. 19, 9); he did not explain this, but it indicates the importance he placed on sexual relationships being within the one marriage.

The Pharisees pointed out that Moses allowed divorce (Matt. 19, 7). Jesus replied that was, "For your hardness of heart" (Matt. 19, 8), suggesting that Moses also opposed it really but he had conceded to a fault in human nature. The relevant Mosaic section (Deuteronomy 24, 1-4) concerns a situation of re-marriage; clearly, divorce is permitted (Deuteronomy 24, 1, 3) and "some indecency" (24, 1) and "dislikes" (24, 3) are given as grounds. There is no hint that Moses regarded divorce as a concession; but whether he did or not, Jesus agreed that he allowed it and Jesus didn't, apart for unchastity. To that extent Jesus virtually overturned if not exactly Moses' law at least the law that was practised in Moses' day- with his acceptance - and thereafter. In arguing that they concurred on the matter basically, Jesus showed his usual support of Moses and his laws, as he solemnly stated in 'the sermon on the mount' (Matt. 5, 17-19) which, I underline, makes his overhauling of some of those laws (e.g. Matt. 5, 38, 39) in the same sermon so surprising. Jesus seemed keen to uphold Moses and all of the prophets.

The sad fact that a marriage might crumble for reasons other than unchastity, leaving divorce as the least grievous option, is not raised in the gospels.

Adultery

Naturally, Jesus forbade adultery (Mk 10, 19; Exodus 20, 14) and he stretched the meaning to include marrying someone else after a divorce (Mk 10, 11, 12), if the dissolution had not been because of unchastity (Matt. 19, 9). Perhaps his thinking was that since divorce was prohibited, except for unchastity, the couple involved remained married regardless; in supposedly marrying another, therefore, they were really having an extra-marital affair. He said that a man who marries a divorced woman commits adultery (Matt. 5, 32; Lk 16, 18) though, it seems to me, the woman would be the obvious one guilty of the offence (Mk 10, 12); and that a man who divorces his wife, apart for unchastity, makes her an adulteress (Matt. 5, 32) - again, to my mind, not unless she remarries, according to Jesus' teaching that adultery includes in its definition divorcing and then at some point marrying another person.

Jesus even extended the meaning to encompass thoughts - "everyone who looks at a woman lustfully has already committed adultery with her in his heart" (Matt. 5, 28). The man might not be married! Possibly Jesus stretched the meaning too far.

Morality: a summary

The fundamental commandments are love God and your neighbour which seems to embrace everyone. But hate sin.

Keep the laws of Moses, though at times, especially during 'the sermon on the mount', Jesus himself changed a few and some of his alterations present incredible demands.

Be concerned about others. Do good deeds as well as refraining from bad ones. Don't have evil thoughts.

In general, Jesus taught that forgiveness is dependent on acknowledgement of wrongdoing.

Love your enemies, but not their faults. Where they sin, try to reform them. Non-resistance may be a particular manifestation of love, but still the aim is to transform the assailant.

Give to the poor, that was Jesus' main instruction. Don't strive to be wealthy; don't be wealthy. The only possession that really matters is a place in the kingdom of God.

Overall Jesus advocated correct judgement, not non-judgement. Perceive our own faults before pointing out those of others.

Live in sincere humility. Practise Jesus' teaching without show. God will notice.

Believers should be totally committed, prepared to leave families and suffer persecution, even to death. They will be rewarded with eternal life.

There should be no divorce except for unchastity. Adultery can include divorce and lust.

Particular
Groups

The Jewish Leaders

Jesus vehemently criticised the Pharisees, Sadducees, chief priests, elders and scribes. He also lambasted the lawyers (Lk 11, 45-52) and referred to Herod the tetrarch as "that fox" (Lk 13, 32). Amongst the accusations he levelled at the leaders were self-righteousness (Lk 18, 11, 12), ignorance of the scriptures (Mk 12, 24), disbelief (Matt. 21, 32), vanity (Lk 20, 45, 46) and hypocrisy (Matt. 23, 2). He particularly labelled them, "hypocrites" (e.g. Matt. 23, 13, 15, 23, 25, 27, 29). They were also, "fools" (Lk 11, 40), "blind guides" (Matt. 15, 14), a "brood of vipers" (Matt. 12, 34), "evil" (Matt. 12, 34), "like white-washed tombs" (Matt. 23, 27), murderers (Matt. 23,35. Com. Jn 8, 44) and children of hell (Matt. 23, 15. Com. Jn 8, 44). Quite a damning catalogue! Where he found fault, Jesus let it be known.

Yet he did not shun the establishment. He answered the problems its representatives posed for him (e.g. Mk 12, 13-17) and he posed some for them (e.g. Matt. 22, 41-45). He had a private conversation with Nicodemus, a Pharisee (Jn 3, 1-15). On occasions Jesus was complimentary, telling the scribe who expounded the first and second commandments that he was "not far from the kingdom of God" (Mk 12, 34); and suggesting that a Pharisee he was dining with, no less, needed only a small amount of forgiveness - though he also showed only a small amount of love (Lk 7, 41-47)! There were other times when Jesus dined with Pharisees (Lk 11, 37-44; 14, 1-6), but in each case both sides criticised each other. They were soon at loggerheads.

Despite the denunciations, Jesus offered his adversaries salvation, depending no doubt on them mending their ways and recognising him as the Son of God - "You search the scriptures, because you think that in them you have eternal life; and it is they that bear witness to me; yet you refuse to come to me that you may have life" (Jn 5, 39, 40). Blistering rebukes, but, as with sinners in general, still the chance to change and be saved.

Gentiles

Gentiles, meaning non-Jews, are given a mixed message in the gospels. At times Jesus speaks quite disparagingly about them - even they salute one another, though only one another (Matt. 5, 47); when praying they "heap up empty phrases" (Matt. 6, 7); they seek physical needs (Matt. 6, 31, 32); his disciples should not order themselves as they do (Lk 22, 25, 26); treat a brother who refuses to acknowledge his fault "as a Gentile" (Matt. 18, 17). Jesus linked them to tax collectors (Matt. 5, 46, 47; 18, 17) whom he demeaned, linking them with harlots (Matt. 21, 31). But he ate with tax collectors (e.g. Mk 2, 15), they believed when the religious leaders didn't (Matt. 21, 32) and one tax collector, Matthew, became a disciple (Matt. 9, 9). Gentiles were taken on a similarly bumpy course.

The barbed comments stated could have been expressions of patriotic bias, found, to some extent, in every nation. For the Jews, though, nationalism ran very deep indeed. They believed that they were God's chosen people (e.g. Genesis 17, 7, 8; Exodus 4, 22; Deuteronomy 7, 6), set apart from others (e.g. Exodus 19, 5; Leviticus 20, 26; Deuteronomy 14, 2) and cared for in particular (e.g. Exodus 3, 7-10; Leviticus 26, 3-13; Deuteronomy 7, 14, 15) - the Old Testament is largely the story of God's relationship with Israel. Jesus too conveyed these convictions. He told the woman of Samaria, "You worship what you do not know; we worship what we know, for salvation is from the Jews" (Jn 4, 22). Jerusalem was "the city of the great King" (Matt. 5, 35). In curing the infirm woman Jesus noted, as though it was a point in her favour, that she was "a daughter of Abraham" (Lk 13, 16); for Zacchaeus, "Today salvation has come to this house since he also is a son of Abraham" (Lk 19, 9). Jesus upheld his people's unique intimacy with God. They were special. When the disciples were sent on a missionary journey they were to "Go nowhere among the Gentiles ... but ... rather to the lost sheep of the house of Israel" (Matt. 10, 5, 6. See, also, Matt. 10, 23). After first ignoring her, Jesus answered the Gentile woman who begged him to cure her daughter by saying he "was sent only to the lost sheep of the house of Israel" (Matt. 15, 24) and he added insult to exclusion by further stating, "It is not fair to take the children's bread and throw it to the dogs" (Matt. 15, 26).

However, "the dogs" statement itself is prefaced by, "Let the children first be fed ..." (Mk 7, 27) - "first", raising the prospect that Gentiles could be second, not that they are excluded altogether, and because of the woman's riposte, Jesus did as she asked. In the sending out of the disciples, there is another somewhat analogous qualification, "rather" (Matt. 10, 6) softens "nowhere" (Matt. 10, 5). Jesus helped the centurion, a Gentile, without any qualms (Matt. 8, 5-7) and he observed that of the ten lepers it was only "this foreigner" (Lk 17, 18), the Samaritan, who returned to give thanks for his healing. He commended all three for their faith, telling the centurion he had not found such "even in Israel" (Matt. 8, 10). Indeed, he implied that many Gentiles would come into the kingdom of heaven whilst the Jews would be "thrown into the outer darkness" (Matt. 8, 11, 12)! So Gentiles can be saved, and faith is more important than race. The rejection of the Jews surfaces again in the parable of The Banquet (Lk 14, 16-24) which seems to be about God's invitation to his people, their excuses, his disowning of them and turning, instead, to the Gentiles. The parable of The Wicked Tenants (Matt. 21, 33-39) certainly makes this point, more dramatically; Jesus draws from it, "Therefore I tell you, the kingdom of God will be taken away from you and given to a nation producing the fruits of it" (Matt. 21, 43). I assume not every Jew will be rejected - what of the disciples themselves? - but no doubt some will, as will some Gentiles. Though at times one or the other, overall both can achieve salvation. God was primarily concerned with his own chosen people, but how someone, anyone, reacts to the gospel determines the outcome.

When addressing the crowds Jesus spoke as though to everyone, Jew and non-Jew alike - "everyone who asks receives" (Matt. 7, 8), "If any man would come after me ..." (Lk 9, 23), "Whoever does the will of God ..." (Mk 3, 35). If he really did intend only the Jews I would expect this to be made more clear more often. "I, when I am lifted up from the earth, will draw all men to myself" (Jn 12, 32) obviously encompasses all of mankind. Again, in the parable of The Wheat and the Weeds (Matt. 13, 24-30) "the field", from which the evil are plucked, represents not Israel but "the world" (Matt. 13, 38); it is "all the nations" who will be separated like "sheep" and "goats" (Matt. 25, 32); the elect will be gathered "from the ends of the earth to the ends of heaven" (Mk 13, 27) and the day of judgement "will come upon all who dwell upon the face of the whole earth" (Lk 21, 35). Quite clearly, then, Gentiles as well as Jews are included and, the readings infer, on the same terms. There is no suggestion of a two - tier judgement. All should hear the conditions, and so Jesus declared, "the gospel must first be preached to all nations" (Mk 13, 10. Com. Matt. 24, 14; 26, 13; Mk 11, 17). His parting words to his disciples were, "repentance and forgiveness of sins should be preached ... to all nations" (Lk 24, 47); "Go ... and make disciples of all nations" (Matt. 28, 19).

In saying he was sent only to "the house of Israel" (Matt. 15, 24), Jesus may have intended that he personally was not to go outside of Israel; in telling the disciples to "Go nowhere among the Gentiles" (Matt. 10, 5) perhaps he was referring to that particular occasion, not to the future; whilst his later declaration that they will not have travelled throughout Israel "before the Son of man comes" (Matt. 10, 23) may mean that he will join them as normal before they have completed that specific mission - though considering the surrounding verses he may indeed mean his final, supernatural coming, and so the world really is omitted. But the indications, some strong, that the gospel is for the Jews only are decisively outweighed by the clear statements and many apparent ones that it is for everyone, believing and practising are what counts. In general outlook Jesus may have viewed Gentiles as second-class citizens - a slant firmly embedded in Judaism - but most often he taught that for entry to the kingdom of God they are on a par with his own nationality.

The Elect

The elect are those "whom he - the Lord - chose" (Mk 13, 20), the righteous ones who will be saved and enter heaven. False prophets will try to lead them "astray" (Matt. 24, 24). But "for the sake of the elect" (Matt. 24, 22) the times of "tribulation" (Matt. 24, 21) will be "shortened" (Matt. 24, 22); they will be vindicated "speedily" (Lk 18, 8), gathered by "the angels" (Mk 13, 27).

On the face of it, these are people who are chosen for their faith and deeds. They have passed God's judgement. However, in the gospels there are shades of another, difficult meaning: the elect have been chosen from the beginning, to become believers at all, they and not others - God decides who is and who isn't to be a believer and, therefore, who is and who isn't to be saved. In John's gospel Jesus refers to those who have been given to him by the Father (Jn 6, 37; 10, 29; 17, 2, 6, 9, 24; 18, 9). This suggests that they themselves are passive, directed by God's will not theirs. But not necessarily! "Given" could mean allows or agrees to, enabling the individual to make the decision to join Jesus and God gives his blessing. The traditional marriage service contains such an idea, roughly, "Who gives this woman to this man?" The woman, I hope, has really made the decision. There are a few more verses which incline towards God predetermining but can be interpreted in other ways. "Every plant which my heavenly Father has not planted will be rooted up" (Matt. 15, 13) could also be rendered as blessing, not causing, and it could refer not to people at all but to the defilement regulation (Matt. 15, 11). Nearby Jesus did indeed compare people to seed (Matt. 13, 3-8, 18-23, 24-30, 37-43) and taught that it is evil forces and not God's will that prevents their salvation. Considering the words "to sit at my right hand and at my left is not mine to grant, but it is for those for whom it has been prepared by my Father" (Matt. 20, 23), "prepared" could refer to the requirements to be met to be able to sit at the right and left, and "those" meaning believers who fulfil the requirements, and not specific, actual characters; or they could simply be recognising that since God knows the future he knows who will in fact occupy those places, by virtue of what they have done of their own accord, not because of what he has programmed them to do. Perhaps the strongest indication that it is God who dictates who believes is, "No one can come to me unless the Father … draws him" (Jn 6, 44). The brevity and imprecision of "draws him" permits some human participation, for example, God prompts someone to listen, but the hearer makes up his own mind. Still, it has to be accepted, God has been involved to some extent and wherever he has compelled someone to do something he, and not the person, is responsible for it. He has determined it.

Given that God knows everything, even the future, and that he can do anything, it is understandable that the notions of divine purpose and control emerge in religion, sometimes within humble praise, perhaps without really thinking through the consequences. There is a note of fatalism. We are but puppets. It's all up to God! Yes, it all depends on his will, but, reason concludes, his will includes our free will. Overwhelmingly Jesus spoke as though the gospel is offered to all and each chooses for himself whether to accept or reject it. So much of his teaching was addressed to the crowds; I refer again to his "everyone" pronouncements. It is apparent that the recipients are responsible for their response, not John 6, 44, but Luke 11, 13, "... how much more will the heavenly Father give the Holy Spirit to those who ask him?" They make the move. The gospels overall read naturally and most sensibly as teaching whether or not to believe is resolved by the individual, not by God. If it was the other way round I would expect such a truly crucial tenet to be unequivocally declared and emphasised, not to be dependent on a few, somewhat ambiguous statements. Surely if only preordained people are admissible to heaven that would have affected the course of Jesus' ministry. He may as well have spoken only to them. He would have known who they were. Why preach to those to whom it made no difference? He could have conducted private conversations, though if those concerned had already been chosen was there any need to speak to them at all? Was there any need for Jesus' ministry? The problem cannot be overcome by proposing that it was only after Jesus' mission that God chose, according to people's reactions - the argument is that the reactions themselves are willed by God.

The concept of God determining in advance who will be saved founders on the essence of justice and of God. Because he knows everything, God knows who will go to heaven, but - the fundamental point - he must be, as it were, a spectator, difficult though that is to envisage, for if he influences, indeed actually ensures, a favourable outcome for some and not others when all are in the same state he is being absolutely unfair. To condemn someone not even born to eventually suffer in hell, to burn, it seems, forever, is as unjust and cruel as I can imagine. Better not to be born at all! The Bible contains examples of God being extremely severe, such as when he destroyed all life on earth except for that on Noah's ark (Genesis 6, 11-8, 19), but it does not portray him as being capricious and malicious. He punishes or rewards for an evidential reason, because of particular actions, and if the people who carried out those actions are not responsible for them they should be neither punished nor rewarded. Justice demands free will. Predestination entails an amount of what we would call evil. I conclude, therefore, that the elect is not the name for those who have been blessed before their lives begin, but for those who have chosen, personally, to be righteous and, on balance, succeeded.

Particular Groups: a summary

Jesus criticised the Jewish leaders in the most scathing terms, and they found fault with him. But he was prepared to mix with them, and on occasions he was complimentary to them. He offered the leaders salvation, if only they would see the light!

At times Jesus was quite disparaging about Gentiles; at times he was quite disparaging about Jews. Overall, though he was particularly interested in God's chosen people, the gospel was for anyone, the criteria the same for all.

There are suggestions that the elect are chosen by God to become believers, but many statements, interpreted naturally, and the implications of predestination on Jesus' ministry and on the nature of justice and of God point to people choosing for themselves. The elect are those who have resolved to be righteous.

What Jesus Didn't Teach About

The existence of God

Jesus and his society took it for granted that God exists. His teachings may raise questions about God (e.g. Lk 13, 1-5) but he had no need to show that there is a god.

Politics

Beyond making a couple of cautionary comments about Herod (Mk 8, 15; Lk 13, 32) and telling Pilate that his "power ... had been given" him "from above" (Jn 19, 11), Jesus did not engage in politics. He appeared to hold that God allowed the present order, and he would have added, for the present. There is no mention of him criticising the Romans; he didn't criticise the Jewish leaders for what they were, but for what they did. He seemed to accept the governance he found around him. Though implying that really he was exempt from taxation (Matt. 17, 25, 26), nonetheless he paid it so as "not to give offence to them" (Matt. 17, 27) and when he was asked about paying taxes to Caesar he replied, "Render ... to Caesar the things that are Caesar's ..." (Matt. 22, 21). Such was the status quo and Jesus obeyed its regulations; his concern lay beyond earthly rules and rulers. They lived in it, but he and his disciples were not of "the world" (Jn 17, 16. Com. Jn 8, 23). "Now is the judgement of this world, now" - meaning really in the near future - "shall the ruler of this world be cast out" (Jn 12, 31) - and replaced by God. Jesus' mission was to prepare people for the kingdom of God, to prompt sinners to repent. Religious, not political!

Turning briefly to modern politics, it is sometimes debated whether Jesus was, in current terminology, a socialist or a capitalist. The parables of The Dishonest Steward (Lk 16, 1-9) and of The Talents (Matt. 25, 14-30) or Pounds (Lk 19, 12-27) trumpet individual enterprise, the latter two applauding the increase of an amount of money and both ending with "to everyone who has will more be given" but "from him who has not, even what he has will be taken away" (Matt. 25, 29; Lk 19, 26). However, though the steward was "commended … for his prudence" (Lk 16, 8), his values are wrong. It is implied that he was a son "of this world" (Lk 16, 8) dealing in "unrighteous mammon" (Lk 16, 9, 11), not "the true riches" (Lk 16, 11); and, as I have argued, the parables of The Talents and The Pounds must be given a religious interpretation, such as increase goodness, or stand in complete contrast to the preponderance of Jesus' teaching about wealth which is, don't be wealthy. Given that riches are not just a danger but an insuperable barrier to salvation, and his emphasis on helping, directly and immediately, the poor and needy, I place Jesus firmly within the socialist fraternity.

Human punishments

Commandment six of the Ten Commandments states, "You shall not kill" (Exodus 20, 13); this really seems to mean, you shall not murder, for warfare was anticipated (e.g. Numbers 1, 1-3) and demanded (e.g. Numbers 31, 1-7) and execution was decreed for a range of offences (e.g. Exodus 21, 12-17; 22, 18-20). I emphasise that Jesus generally upheld the Mosaic law.

He cited human punishments in his teaching. His parables include imprisonment "till he should pay all his debt" (Matt. 18, 34) and death to those who killed the servants sent to invite them to a marriage feast (Matt. 22, 7) and to those who killed the servants and the son sent to collect some of the produce of the vineyard (Mk 12, 9). Of course, parables are to be interpreted and the penalties meted out probably stand for God's sentences, but within the stories themselves the crimes are atrocious and the punishments read as deserved and heartfelt - "What will the owner of the vineyard do? He will come and destroy the tenants …" (Mk 12, 9). This comes across as a just response amongst men as well as standing for divine retribution. I notice the strength of the word "destroy", suggesting personal feeling, and Jesus does not indicate that he is simply observing how men in fact react. In the parable of The Faithful and Unfaithful Steward (Lk 12, 42-46), the master likely stands for Jesus, the event, his second coming, and the unfaithful servant is condemned to hell. But Jesus appears to extend the story into a human situation when he says one servant "shall receive a severe beating" (Lk 12, 47) and another "a light beating" (Lk 12, 48). Again, he may be stating no more than what will actually happen, or he may be saying what he considers should happen. Certainly he does not show any disapproval of it.

Outside of the parables altogether Jesus warned of imprisonment "till you have paid the last penny" (Matt. 5, 26), and the only lesson he drew from Pilate killing Galileans (Lk 13, 1) was not that it was bad, but "unless you repent you will all likewise perish" (Lk 13, 3). When he was about to be stoned, Jesus did not object that the action itself was wrong, but asked for which of his "good works" was he to be so treated (Jn 10, 31, 32); when Pilate pointed out that he had the power to crucify him, Jesus expressed no dissent about sentencing someone to death or about the manner of the execution, but replied only that Pilate's power came "from above" (Jn 19, 10, 11).

Whilst these facts and inferences do not establish that Jesus agreed with human punishments, not criticising them when he may well have done so, the tendencies, forceful vocabulary and emotive feel of his statements relating to the matter, and God, through Moses, specifying crimes and penalties on earth, all incline towards his agreement.

Suicide

The Old Testament contains two famous cases of suicide - Samson (Judges 16, 29, 30) and Saul (1 Samuel 31, 4; assisted suicide, 2 Samuel 1, 9, 10); the New Testament, one - Judas Iscariot (Matt. 27, 5). In each case no comment is made about the rights or wrongs of the action itself. There is not a Pentateuchal law on suicide, and Jesus says nothing about it.

When Job learnt of the deaths of his servants and his children he responded with, "the Lord gave, and the Lord has taken away" (Job 1, 21). These words have been generalised into "the Lord gives and the Lord takes away" and moralised into "because God gives only he has the right to take away". On the other hand it is reasoned that giving to us necessarily implies becoming ours. Moreover, God wants us to choose the course of our lives. He also gives free will and that includes the freedom to end one's own life. What Jesus thought about the matter, if he thought about it at all, is unknown.

Abortion

The Bible does not raise the topic. It does maintain that God creates every person (e.g. Job 31, 15; Ecclesiastes 11, 5; Isaiah 44, 2; Jeremiah 1, 5). It can be said, therefore, that abortion interferes with his creation; so does every medical procedure and, indeed, every physical action. But abortion deliberately ends a potential life. We are told that when Mary greeted Elizabeth "the babe in my womb leaped for joy" (Lk 1, 44. See, also, Isaiah 49, 1) which could be used as evidence that foetus' are aware of the outside world. Whether or not anti-abortionists go as far as this, they do emphasise that an embryo is to some extent alive, and they appeal to compassion and justice - it is wrong to end an innocent life, perhaps any life. On the other side it may be claimed that pre-natal existence amounts to mechanics, that a person only becomes one at birth, and that there are circumstances where more good than harm is done by terminating a pregnancy - for instance, rape, and if the health, perhaps the very life, of the mother is endangered. The issue produces many conflicting values. Jesus did not mention it and for me his teaching provides no guidelines one way or the other.

Servitude

Five times in the gospels Jesus uses a word which could be translated as "slave" or "servant" (Matt. 10, 24; 13, 27; Jn 13, 16; 15, 15, twice) and on none of these occasions does he object to what it stands for. He taught "whoever would be first among you must be your slave" (Matt. 20, 27) and "a servant" is not "above his master"

(Matt. 10, 24. Com. Jn 13, 16). Indeed, a servant should attend to his master's needs first and not expect to be thanked for doing his duty (Lk 17, 7-9), and men should serve God similarly (Lk 17, 10). What a servant can expect is to be treated properly (Lk 17, 8b; 12, 42, 45, 46). Jesus did not discuss one person serving another in principle, but, as illustrated, where he did refer to the practice he spoke of it as normal and conveyed no personal disquiet. He did not reproach the centurion for having a slave (Lk 7, 2) or repudiate the bond when he healed the slave of the high priest (Lk 22, 50, 51).

The law of Moses permitted slavery (e.g. Leviticus 25, 44-46) and set out its regulations (e.g. Exodus 21, 1-11), so Jesus was likely to say the same. Paul instructed, "Slaves, obey in everything those who are your earthly masters" (Colossians 3, 22); "Masters, treat your slaves justly and fairly" (Colossians 4, 1). If Jesus had censured slavery, and Paul knew it, he would hardly have delivered these injunctions.

Jesus speaking of servitude, including slavery, only in terms of a working relationship and comparing it, as a model, to man and God and, further, Moses' and Paul's endorsements of and prescriptions for slavery, strongly suggest that Jesus himself accepted the custom. The indications are that he approved of it. Certainly, he did not seem to find it disturbing.

Homosexuality

The Old Testament denounced homosexuality as "an abomination" (Leviticus 18, 22), to be punished by death (Leviticus 20, 13). I say again that Jesus normally upheld Moses' commands.

Jesus himself specifically condemned adultery (Matt. 19, 18), fornication (Mk 7, 21) and licentiousness (Mk 7, 22), and I see no reason why he would not have added homosexuality to his list of "evil things" (Mk 7, 23). He reminded his hearers of the fate of Sodom (Matt. 11, 23. See, especially, Genesis 19, 4-8, 24).

Paul declared that homosexuals will not "inherit the kingdom of God" (1 Corinthians 6, 9, 10). He wrote of women indulging in "unnatural" relations and men behaving likewise, "consumed with passion for one another … and receiving … the due penalty for their error" (Romans 1, 26, 27) - judgements not to be passed without the surety of Jesus' assent.

Women

Jesus said nothing in particular about women. In the few references to them in his teaching (e.g. Matt. 13, 33; 24, 41) they are mainly in domestic situations, and so they are usually placed in the gospels. Some women seem to have been very useful to Jesus and his disciples "ministering to him" (Matt. 27, 55) and providing "for them out of their means" (Lk 8, 3).

The disciples "marvelled" when they found Jesus "talking with a woman" (Jn 4, 27). In fact he had a long conversation with her (Jn 4, 7-26). He allowed another to anoint him (Mk 14, 3). He seemed to be quite at home with Martha and Mary (Lk 10, 38-42; Jn 11, 5, 28, 32-35; 12, 2). If Jesus did not often speak to women this might have been out of propriety rather than disinclination.

Twice he called his own mother "woman" (Jn 2, 4; 19, 26) and he sometimes said the same when referring to others (Matt. 15, 28; 26, 10; Lk 13, 12, 16). I have been told that in the Middle East to call a lady "woman" does not carry the rude connotation we would associate with it. Jesus' speech in the gospels is generally impersonal which is natural since what is recorded are not casual tete-a-tetes, but, for the most part, teachings addressed to his disciples collectively, to the crowds and to strangers.

The gospel message is the same for men and women. Jesus made no distinction. He praised the faith of the woman who had a haemorrhage (Mk 5, 34) and of the Canaanite one (Matt. 15, 28) and he granted their wishes. He forgave the sinful woman (Lk 7, 48). Mary, he said, had "chosen the good portion" which would "not be taken away from her" (Lk 10, 42), and he told the Samaritan that if she had asked he would have given her "living water" (Jn 4, 10). Of the two women grinding at the mill, one is saved (Matt. 24, 41), an outcome one may anticipate between men.

A topical issue is, can women be leaders in the church? It is frequently pointed out that all of Jesus' twelve disciples were men. This may have been because he thought that only men were suitable or because he was following custom - men were usually in positions of authority - or because such was the way events transpired, these were the people he came across and accepted. We don't know. Jesus never explained the fact and he did not say if women could become officials. Apart from his closing words suggesting he wanted Peter to lead the believers in the future (Jn 21, 15-17), Jesus did not say how they were to organise themselves. There was no real need. No thorough organisation was necessary. The future would be short. He envisaged not a settled, ordered church but evangelism and persecution (e.g. Mk 13) until in the lifetime of his own generation (e.g. Mk 13, 30) he returned to establish the kingdom of God.

Though he also expected Jesus to return in his lifetime (1 Corinthians 15, 51; 1 Thessalonians 4, 15), Paul sanctioned some structure in the church. He referred to "the office of bishop" (1 Timothy 3, 1) and "Deacons" (1 Timothy 3, 8), and he commended Phoebe, "a deaconess" (Romans 16, 1), presumably the female equivalent of a deacon. He did not spell out the latter's duties - distributing alms? (see Acts 6, 1-6) - but he seemed to agree with a woman having some formal role in Christianity. I assume he did not think Jesus would disagree.

Soldiers

"Do not resist one who is evil. But if anyone strikes you on the right cheek, turn to him the other also" (Matt. 5, 39). So, do not fight. Therefore do not be a soldier. Impeccable! Yet I am unconvinced. Does the quotation really refer to everyday person to person conduct? Whoever is intended, is it hyperbole? As noted, Jesus himself assaulted the traders in the temple (Jn 2, 14-16), he certainly resisted evil verbally and he complained when he was struck (Jn 18, 22, 23). The real message may be, strive to live in peace with each other.

Even "all who take the sword will perish by the sword" (Matt. 26, 52) might not have had soldiers in mind but, and especially given the context, been a general warning against violence. Clearly, though, the statement does encompass the military and counts against it; clearly, too, "all" makes it incorrect, as Jesus would have known as much as anybody. It is not inevitable that a soldier will die violently; many die naturally.

When he met the centurion (Matt. 8, 5-13), Jesus did not criticise his profession. It has been observed that he never told a soldier to stop being one, so far as we know. There was an occasion when he spoke of armed force in a very practical manner and without any moral comment (Lk 14, 31, 32). What is lacking is a definite pronouncement on the subject. Jesus predicted wars (Matt. 24, 6), "nation will rise against nation" (Matt. 24, 7). Wars imply armies, so he envisaged the continued use of soldiers. He wanted peace, not war (e.g. Matt. 5, 9), but perhaps he accepted that a mixture was the way of this world and would be until all conflict was resolved in God's world.

Animals

The law commanded help if a person came across an ox or an ass that had wandered or fallen (Exodus 23, 4, 5); perhaps this was more for the sake of the owner than the animal - "so you shall do with his ass; so you shall do with his garment; so you shall do with any lost thing of your brother's …" (Deuteronomy 22, 3). Like a garment, a "beast" (Exodus 22, 10) was "property" (Exodus 22, 11). If you find a bird's nest and a mother with her young, you may take the young but not the mother (Deuteronomy 22, 6, 7), possibly out of consideration for the mother or for some reason such as she might have more offspring. Don't "muzzle an ox when it treads out the grain" (Deuteronomy 25, 4); again the reason might be out of regard for the ox or, for example, that muzzling slows down its work rate.

On this verse Paul commented, "Is it for oxen that God is concerned? Does he not speak entirely for our sake? It was written for our sake ..." (1 Corinthians 9,9, 10). I can't think of any verse which clearly suggests care for animals for their own sakes because they are sentient beings. It seems that they were there to be used - worked, sacrificed, eaten.

Jesus probably concurred with this outlook. He ate meat (Mk 14, 14. See Exodus 12, 1-13) and sanctioned sacrifices (Mk 1, 44. See Leviticus 14, 1-32). His only close association with a living animal was when he rode a colt into Jerusalem (Mk 11, 1-11). He spoke of God feeding the birds (Matt. 6, 26; Lk 12, 24), presumably meaning God providing plants and insects which birds eat, and of God deciding their demise (Matt. 10, 29) and not forgetting them when they are bandied about (Lk 12, 6). But in what manner does he remember them? The point became that men are more valuable than they are (Matt. 6, 26; 10, 13; Lk 12, 7, 24). Did God or Jesus really care about the birds? "Are not five sparrows sold for two pennies?" (Lk 12,6) was asked without any hint of disapproval. Were they rather like the grass "which today is alive and tomorrow is thrown into the oven" (Matt. 6, 30)? "Do not give dogs what is holy" (Matt. 7, 6) indicates their inferiority; "do not throw your pearls before swine, lest they trample them under foot and turn to attack you" (Matt. 7, 6) warns of their bestiality. Both remarks lack any warmth or recognition of innate limitations or of meritorious features. Jesus gave permission for "demons" (Matt. 8, 31) to enter "about two thousand" (Mk 5, 13) pigs who then "rushed ... into the sea, and were drowned" (Mk 5, 13). No concern there for the pigs; instead, a favour to the demons! There is no evident affection for animals anywhere in the gospels. A different, but still a living species was the fig tree which Jesus cursed because he didn't find any fruit on it (Mk 11, 12-14, 20) - unpleasant, and unjust since "it was not the season for figs" (Mk 11, 13).

Topics not taught: a summary

It was taken for granted that God exists.

Jesus was not political. He seemed to accept the status quo. Soon, however, all would change; his preoccupation was to prepare people for the new, everlasting order.

Though he did not pronounce on human punishments, it is likely that Jesus agreed with the practice.

He said nothing at all about suicide or abortion.

Slavery was normal, and it appears that Jesus accepted it.

He probably would have condemned homosexuality.

The gospel was as much for women as for men. Jesus did not indicate whether a woman could hold a position of authority.

Soldiers were part of the present structure. The morality of their purpose was not specifically addressed.

Animals were useful. There are no perceptible feelings for them themselves.

A personal perspective

Given that the Bible is the fount of Christianity, one fundamental question is, how much of the Bible does a Christian accept? Though consisting of many books by many authors, it is commonly spoken of as all the word of God, so accept it all. Then what of the problems, the conflicting and puzzling accounts and statements? There are two versions of creation, side by side, in Genesis chapters 1 and 2. Why should Cain build "a city" (Genesis 4, 17) when there were only five people on earth? Did David or Elhanan slay Goliath (1 Samuel 17, 49; 2 Samuel 21, 19; 1 Samuel 17, 7; 1 Chronicles 20, 5)? Given that God is perfect, all-knowing, why should he repent and change his mind (Genesis 6, 6; Exodus 32, 14; 1 Samuel 15, 35, contrast 1 Samuel 15, 29; Jonah 3, 10)? In the gospels the nativity and resurrection accounts differ in many details. Was Jesus crucified at "the third hour" (Mk 15, 25) or "about the sixth hour" (Jn 19, 14)? Who are the "we" in John chapter 21 verse 24 and in the first half of Acts chapter 16? What of the godly acting out of character - David killing every person who witnessed his raids (1 Samuel 27, 8-11), Jesus cursing a fig tree (Mk 11, 14), Paul blinding an opponent (Acts 13, 6-11. Contrast 1 Thessalonians 5,15)?

The nature and range of miracles are likely to divide opinion. Are they all credible? If some and not others, why? Is Joshua ordering the sun to stand still (Joshua 10, 12-14) or Elisha making an iron axe head float (2 Kings 6, 4-7) as believable as Jesus curing the sick? Consider, too, scientific discoveries such as evolution and historical inaccuracies such as in the book of Daniel, especially regarding the Babylonian and Persian kings.

I think nearly everyone would agree with some of Moses' laws, but how many would support, if you do not redeem the first-born of an ass "you shall break its neck" (Exodus 34, 20) or if a wife is suspected of adultery she should drink dirty water to see if her body swells up (Numbers 5, 11- 28) or "If a man takes a wife and her mother also ... they shall be burned" (Leviticus 20, 14)? Who is content with God punishing children for their fathers' iniquities (Exodus 34, 7. Contrast Deuteronomy 24, 16) or with him commanding, through Moses, genocide (e.g. Deuteronomy 20,16-18. Com. Joshua 6, 21; 8, 1, 2)?

So, perhaps, accept not all, but parts of the Bible. Which parts? Why? There could be as many variations as there are people. "That many men, that many opinions". By definition God cannot be wrong. Therefore any passage which someone does not accept cannot be, in their judgement, the word of God. Human fallibility has crept in. For a Christian the crucial portion of the Bible is that which describes the life and teachings of Jesus Christ - the four gospels. As I have propounded, page after page, these too have their problems. A Christian must find the way through the maze that is most satisfactory to him. He could attribute faults to the writers or their sources, providing he does not maintain that God is the real author. He might conclude that sometimes Jesus himself spoke imprecisely or inconsistently, providing he does not maintain that as the Son of God, Jesus could no more make a mistake than God himself. It may be that the Bible in its entirety has not been revealed or dictated - though it could still be inspired - by God, but is the work of men writing within their own culture about their Lord, his prophets, his particular people and the rest of the world. This view admits differences, forgetfulness, loose phrasing, errors and personal assessments and inclina- tions - for example, the righteousness of Samuel, the sin- fulness of Saul (e.g. 1 Samuel 15, 35), Luke's emphasis on the poor, John's on believing in Jesus. Seeing that the teachings are presented not as a carefully reasoned, inter-locking treatise but as a collection of impromptu pieces, short and long, there are likely to be inconsistencies. My approach has been that we do not know which of the statements apparently spoken by Jesus really were spoken by him, so I have allowed for all of them, and searched, in each subject area, for the predominant theme, hoping that is what he really meant.

If we love anyone as much as ourselves then, frankly, it is probably no more than one or two others. These are the people who are extremely dear to us, who we think and care about daily. But we can consider everyone, bearing in mind their likes and dislikes, as we do our own, and we can help them, to some extent, in times of trouble. This, I have proposed, is the kind of love Jesus had in mind. Be concerned, not consumed! Love does not entail allowing anything, condoning everything that gives satisfaction. Jesus taught that many thoughts and actions are simply bad and if a person persists in badness he will be punished - probably immersed in fire, forever! But a sinner can repent and in most cases he will be for-given. Thus God shows his love and in response to wrongdoing men can show theirs, not by overlooking, but by understanding, weighing 'pros' against 'cons', reflecting on circumstances and background. Granted that love does not necessarily imply giving way to the wishes of those concerned, then it is not the answer to some of the "topics not taught about". It does not, on its own, forbid human punishments and slavery and permit suicide, homosexuality and women becoming priests. Love demands a careful hearing and considera-tion of those affected, but the answers lie in the teaching and if there is no specific teaching one searches for indications - if none can be found, then one can turn to non-gospel criteria.

It seems reasonable to suppose that love does not permit cruelty, but the deliberate inflicting of pain, mental, physical or both, is an intrinsic component of punishment and, I have argued, Jesus would probably have endorsed human punishments. He definitely warned of God's horrific penalties. Slavery does not have to be cruel. I suspect our own view of the relationship has been coloured by the brutal African - European slave trade of, predominately, the 17th and 18th Centuries. The Hebrew version was milder (e.g. Exodus 21, 2-11, 20, 21, 26, 27). Jesus taught that the steward should give the household "their portion of food at the proper time" and if he began to beat the servants, perhaps without cause, he would be punished (Lk 12, 42-46).

Love alone does not fill the gaps. But there are other ideals - equality, freedom and human rights. So, for example, freedom renders slavery impossible, equality ensures women can apply for any position, and we have a right to end our own lives. The great snag is, these are not Biblical ideals. Jesus was a religious and moral teacher, not a political and social revolutionary. To me he comes across as a man of his age, conforming to the basic attitudes and conventions he found around him, and if the Mosaic code gave guidance he most likely upheld it. He did not espouse human rights, freedom, democracy or equality except to teach, overall, that the gospel was for everyone and everyone would be judged by the same standards. The Pentateuch commanded and detailed human punishments, including capital punishment, permitted slavery and prohibited homosexuality, and I have surmised that Jesus would have assented to each of these precepts. If a Christian agrees with my conclusion he should assent too because his beliefs are those of Christ. Concepts such as equality and freedom are extremely appealing. They are prevalent and it is natural that a citizen wishes to fit into his society. But a Christian's overwhelming allegiance is to Christ. It is his desire and duty to practise his teaching. In any situation he should ask, what would Jesus have thought and done? I must try to do the same. Moreover, human values change. God, on the other hand, does not need to move with the times. His omniscience means that he knows all that is in store; he is aware of everything when making his decrees. The psalmist wrote, "The law of the Lord is perfect" (Psalm 19, 7) and Jesus stated that it would stand "until all is accomplished" (Matt. 5, 18). If the laws *were* changed, who is to say so? For a Christian the only eligible person is Jesus and he did indeed change a few, but where he didn't they stand as binding today as they were yesterday; likewise the indications we infer from his words and conduct, and so they will continue "till heaven and earth pass away" (Matt. 5, 18).

Recently, in the name of equality, the protection of minorities has been emphasised. "Anti-hate" legislation has been introduced. "Racist" and "sexist" are terms much in vogue. Within my lifetime homosexuals have moved from being abnormal to normal, from disgusting to laudable; now, woe betide anyone who doesn't approve of them. A boxer expressed his thought that homosexuality should still be criminalised, and for saying so he was threatened with removal from a sports-man of the year competition. He was, apparently, homo-phobic, a dreadful condition! How about, individualistic, not so dreadful? Remember freedom of speech? Insults and harassment, no! Personal opinions, yes!

To disagree with homosexuality has proved truly costly for some Christians because of the blanket demand for equal treatment. I understand that a magistrate, a Christian, was dismissed because he maintained that children should be brought up by heterosexual couples only. Presumably the law stipulates that all couples must be given the same opportunity and therefore one cannot start with a preference for, let alone an insistence upon, mixed couples. So the magistrate could simply have been excused officiating in relevant cases. Particularly under pressure are Christians who do not concur with homosexuality and who work in the retail and hospitality sectors. A shopkeeper was found guilty of discrimination because she would not sell flowers to a same-sex couple. This encounter was so routine, fleeting and impersonal, I am unsure whether she should have refused. But I am convinced that Christians who are expected to contribute, in a significant way, to homosexual relationships should have the right to say no. Some bakers who were Christians were prosecuted, successfully, because they were not prepared to inscribe "support gay marriage" on a cake. The law required them to actively promote a cause their religion required them to repudiate. The proprietors of a bed and breakfast residence were penalised for not allowing a homosexual pair to share the same bedroom. They would accommodate them, but in separate rooms. The owners - Christians - were concerned that the two would conduct a proscribed sexual act on their premises. They would be facilitating sin. Not the law, but as good as for those concerned, was the decision by the management of a National Trust property that its employees had to wear a shirt supporting same-sex relationships if they were to perform front-line duties. Thankfully the order was rescinded. It seems that society has moved from one extreme to near the opposite; today it is those who oppose homosexuality who are vilified.

Sometimes I come across notices stating, "The management reserves the right to refuse admission," and thereby refuses to supply whatever is normally available. There are then some circumstances where members of the public can be denied a service. Surely religious belief should be a valid reason for withdrawing unacceptably significant aspects of participation. There is at least the exception that clergy are not obliged to marry same-sex pairs if they would rather not. More provisos are required. Perhaps a balance could be found to the effect that a Christian who objects to homosexuality and who offers a service should perform his basic work for all so long as it does not involve a specific enhancement of homosexuality. Even so, in some cases non-participation could necessitate not serving at all - a printer refused to print homosexual literature, and was arraigned. My proposal might amount to selling products which are on display, insisting on separate rooms and such like; anything more would entail a meaningful support of wrongdoing, as perceived, and the law should recognise this all-important reservation, and protect it.

I have mentioned same-sex marriage. The very idea of two males or two females marrying is, according to the Oxford Dictionary I possess, impossible since marriage is a union of a man and a woman, and if some appropriately updated definition is applied instead, still homosexual wedlock would be impermissible for many Christians because of the sexual implications. The Bible takes for granted that marriage is between members of the opposite sex and that has been mankind's understanding of the word throughout the ages. The Oxford Dictionary states that a usual purpose of marriage is procreation, as does the church. A male and a female are needed to "Be fruitful and multiply" (Genesis 1, 28), a biological condition which no quantity of legislation can overcome; and in multiplying they form a natural, balanced family. There were civil partnerships but the parliament of the day decided - in its rush to dismantle gender - that they were not equal enough, and exercising its prerogative to pass any statute it pleases, it changed the meaning of marriage. This was much more than "tidying up" the law as the Prime Minister described it - and he a man who also proclaimed the importance of the Christian heritage. What he did was to trample upon God's design, as presented in the Old Testament (e.g. Genesis 2, 20-24) and underlined in the New (e.g. Mk 10, 6-8), and upon a concept, a definition and a tradition which had held since the relationship was conceived - and he a Conservative!

Christians who disagree with homosexuality regard it as a sin and therefore wish that it did not exist. If they conclude that Jesus agreed with Moses' prohibition of it, they too should want it prohibited. But I dare say there are many who would not go to this point, perhaps because they are not so convinced or for a reason such as they are more swayed by the concept of choice and its place in the gospels. Homosexuality is a lifestyle, not a blatantly anti-social action. Jesus' response to acts of sin was not usually to threaten those committing them with men's courts but with God's judgement. He told sinners to repent, but they made the choice, receive or reject the message (e.g. Lk 10, 8-12). Similarly, the Christians I have in mind register their disapproval of same-sex relationships and, showing their concern, their love, they try to induce those involved to change their ways, but they leave them to decide. They are civil to, indeed friendly with, homosexuals. Let's recall that Jesus ate with sinners (Mk 2, 15-17). Constant pressure might make matters worse. For their part homosexuals too could, and hopefully many do, respect the right of personal choice, including the religious stance outlined. These days the law appears to be almost totally on their side, but there is no need to rub it in. They do not have to take advantage of every situation, pursuing it through the courts. Faced by a Christian anxious not to collaborate in what he sincerely and profoundly believes to be sinful, a homosexual could be sensitive enough to move on. There are other B. and B's, other bakeries and other relationships as deep as marriage but without the name. I say, live and let live, all-round!

Jesus' teaching and Old Testament teaching

Jesus was in the tradition of the Old Testament prophets in proclaiming repent, be righteous and be saved (e.g. Leviticus 26, 40-42; Deuteronomy 4, 30, 31; 1 Samuel 7, 3; Isaiah 30, 19-26; Jeremiah 4, 14; Ezekiel 18, 21, 30-32; Daniel 9, 24; Hosea 6, 1; Joel 2, 12, 13; Jonah 3, 10. See, also, Amos 5, 14; Malachi 3, 7). Two common Old Testament themes are obey and thrive (e.g. Leviticus 26, 3-12; Deuteronomy 28, 1-14; 1 Samuel 12, 14; Isaiah 1, 19; Jeremiah 11, 3-5); don't obey and suffer (e.g. Leviticus 26, 14-20; Numbers 32, 15; Isaiah 1, 20; Jeremiah 32, 22, 23; Ezekiel 33, 29). A form of suffering often mentioned is conquest by foreigners (e.g. 1 Samuel

12, 9; Isaiah 10, 5,6; Jeremiah 25, 8, 9; Ezekiel 7, 23, 24; Amos 6, 14), but the chastening over, God would rescue his people and they would live righteously and, therefore, in safety and prosperity (e.g. Deuteronomy 30, 1-3, 7-9; 1 Samuel 12, 11; Isaiah 30, 19-26; Jeremiah 50, 17-20; Ezekiel 28, 24-26; Joel 2, 20, 25, 26).

The prelude to this new, blissful age would be "the day of the Lord" (see Isaiah 2, 12-19), "near" (Joel 3, 14) and in itself "bitter" (Zephaniah 1, 14) because there would be punishment, sometimes of the conquerors now turned "oppressors" (e.g. Zephaniah 3, 19. See Isaiah 10, 12; Jeremiah 50, 18; Zephaniah 3, 15; Zechariah 14, 12), sometimes of everyone and everything (e.g. Isaiah 24, 3; Nahum 1, 5; Zephaniah 1, 2, 3, 18. See, also, Ezekiel 21, 3; Amos 9, 1), and sometimes, more reasonably, of sinners, in Israel (e.g. Zephaniah 1, 7-9; Malachi 4, 1 ? Note "sons of Jacob", Malachi 3, 6) and throughout the Earth (e.g. Isaiah 13, 9; Jeremiah 25, 31; Obadiah 1, 15). "The Lord will judge the world with righteousness" (Psalm 96, 13). The pattern of sin, punishment, repentance and redemption could be cyclical (n.b. Jeremiah 50, 17) but the later prophets came to see the day of the Lord as final and the new age as glorious and eternal (e.g. Isaiah 9, 7; Jeremiah 31, 38-40; Ezekiel 37, 24-28; Joel 2, 26, 27; Micah 4, 6, 7).

Jesus expressed some of these ideas, but he spoke not of foreigners who had mistreated Israel, but of sinners in general, and indeed not predominantly of Israel at all, but the world; not be faithful and have a good earthly life, but be faithful and have a good afterlife. He may have thought the Roman occupation was retribution sent by God on a wayward nation, but the gospels do not record him saying so. He did not look to an exemplary Israel shining amongst and drawing to it other nations (contrast Isaiah 2, 2, 3) but, simply, to one kingdom ruled by God. Jesus urged people, everybody, to be righteous, ready for "that day" (Mk 13, 32), the day of the Lord, for the coming of the divine realm. His vision was cosmic; like Isaiah (13, 10) and Joel (3, 15), he foresaw the sun, the moon and the stars failing (Mk 13, 24, 25). Then he, as God's representative, would approach the Earth and his angels would gather the worthy, those alive at the time and those raised from the dead (see Isaiah 26, 19; Job 19, 25-27) and bring them into Heaven, whilst condemning the unworthy to Hell (com. Daniel 12, 1, 2).

Rooted in the Old Testament was the belief that a restored Israel would be ruled by a great king (e.g. Isaiah 9, 6, 7; Jeremiah 23, 5, 6; Ezekiel 37, 24, 25; Hosea 3, 5; Micah 5, 2; Zechariah 9, 9), titled The Messiah (Hebrew, 'the anointed one') or The Christ (Greek, 'Christos'). People in the gospels anticipate this figure (e.g. Matt. 2, 1-4; Lk 2,25, 26; Jn 4, 25; 12, 34). Jesus identified himself as The Messiah (e.g. Matt. 16, 15-17). Hence, Jesus the Christ - Jesus Christ - Christians - Christianity. He did indeed pinpoint Israel, but his primary focus was the world. As granted by God, he was to rule a new Earth. His messiahship was twofold: first he came to proclaim the message; next he would come to disclose who had obeyed it - first, the preacher; next, the judge; throughout, the king.

Lightning Source UK Ltd.
Milton Keynes UK
UKHW01f1446181018

330774UK00001B/4/P